CHASING DOWN *the* DAWN

Also by Jewel

A Night Without Armor

CHASING DOWN *the* DAWN

WRITTEN &
ILLUSTRATED
BY JEWEL
KILCHER

HarperEntertainment
An Imprint of HarperCollins*Publishers*

CHASING DOWN THE DAWN. Copyright © 2000 by Jewel Kilcher. All rights reserved. Printed in the United States of America. No part of this book may be used or reproduced in any manner whatsoever without written permission except in the case of brief quotations embodied in critical articles and reviews. For information address HarperCollins Publishers Inc., 10 East 53rd Street, New York, NY 10022.

HarperCollins books may be purchased for educational, business, or sales promotional use. For information please write: Special Markets Department, HarperCollins Publishers Inc., 10 East 53rd Street, New York, NY 10022.

FIRST EDITION

Designed by Berne Smith

Illustrations by Jewel Kilcher

Library of Congress Cataloging-in-Publication Data
Jewel, 1974–
  Chasing down the dawn / Jewel.
      p. cm.
    ISBN 0-06-019200-3
    1. Jewel, 1974– 2. Rock musicians—United States—Biography

  ML420.J38 A3 2000
  782.42164′092—dc 21   00-059685
  [B]

00 01 02 03 04 ❖/RRD 10 9 8 7 6 5 4 3 2 1

www.jeweljk.com

To those who have taught me with such grace
and loved me with such constancy

. . . These are the things which made me
these are the things I call home
these are the things that have filled
my heart with song and I raise them now in homage:

my father and I riding until after dark
chasing cattle or startling eagles into flight
cooking on a coal stove
cutting meat with a dull knife
my hands raw from picking rose hips
on the sea cliffs above Kachemak Bay
staring endlessly at the blue sky . . .

I will return to you, Alaska,
my beloved, but for now
I am youth's soldier
       chasing down
    an endless dawn.

—Jewel, "The Slow Migration of Glaciers,"
from *A Night Without Armor*

Acknowledgments

I would like to thank many people for their help with this book. Barbara Lagowski for her tenacity in tackling the large task of reading, organizing, and helping sort through countless pages of handwritten manuscript. Berne Smith for his help with the complete layout of the book, from fonts to photographs.

Thanks to Nedra Carroll, Dean Thompson, David Owen Kniffen, Ken Calhoun, Colleen Anderson, and Barbara Lagowski for our editing powwows, debating such important points as "Is there another word for 'keening'? Maybe 'grievous moaning'? 'Intense anguish'? 'Deep sorrow, vocally expressed'?" Gratitude to West Kennerly for committing it to film, Francesca San Diego for connecting all the dots, and Cambria Jensen for her persistent proofreading. Also, my appreciation to Rick Mumma and Jeanette Lagowski for typing.

I would like to thank my mom, Nedra, for her continued and boundless support, and my dad, Atz Kilcher, for his support as well. I appreciate his pride in and acceptance of my work.

Finally, I'd like to thank HarperCollins and my editor, Mauro DiPreta.

A Note from Jewel

Chasing Down the Dawn was written primarily on the road during the *Spirit* World Tour. It is a series of short stories and vignettes written in hotel rooms, backstage holding pens, airports, buses, and quiet moments. I wrote some of the stories specifically for the book, while others are excerpts from my journal. They all reflect observations and feelings about the life I've come from and the life I find myself in now.

A variety of voices, time frames, and moods inhabit the stories—echoes from the past and the child I have been, echoes from the future, and sketches of the present. There is no chronological structure. The writing reflects a stream of consciousness, like stepping into the rhythm of my mind as it mirrors my life in a nonlinear way.

Much like a mosaic, when placed together the many small pieces expose a view of my life in a larger sense, revealing a feel for my thought process, my passions and motivations.

CHAPTER *1*

The matter has nothing to do with position or place. There are a million ways to lack courage, whether you are rich or poor, and just as many ways to be heroic. I know that now.

On a Private Plane Headed to Minneapolis

It is nearly winter. Summer has passed so quickly. Summer is the best time to be in Alaska. I remember those lovely summer months and lazy days when the endless daylight beckoned us deep into the woods to lie on our backs and stare at the sky. Now it is cold and the hills will be covered in ice.

Winter could be challenging. The long, dark months confining us to our cabin. Our nerves growing raw from living elbow to elbow. Overnight, the coal stove would burn out, leaving the house to absorb the rock-hard cold of the frozen yard. I'd open my eyes to discover that the picture window that overlooked the meadows was covered in paisley patterns of frost. On particularly cold mornings I would wake to find my brothers sleeping soundly, a faint trace of white frost icing their eyelashes where the white puffs of their breath had condensed and settled.

There were fun times amid the chores and difficulties. A couple times a year we hitched our roan horse, Nikka, to the sleigh and tied jingle bells to the sideboards and my dad would drive us two miles through the snowy meadows to the road where we'd wait for the bus that would take us to school and town. We were the only kids, except for the Rainwaters maybe, who got driven to school in a jingle sleigh. The music of the bells filled my ears and all the empty valleys. On the way home my dad would pick us up on the sleigh with toboggans in tow, and he and the boys would make a mile-long toboggan run through meadow after meadow, ducking under the barbed-wire fences that separated pastures. I'd get to drive the horse and sleigh the whole way home in the dwindling daylight, while the others enjoyed sledding. Or if my dad drove, I would straddle the leather harnesses and ride Nikka bareback, nothing between me and the frosty tundra. The mountains white, with their glaciers spreading like frozen wings. The tall spruce trees covered in sugar, the meadows and mute fields, crosshatched with neat trails that the cows and horses followed religiously to water holes.

The bay was beautiful but eerie in the winter. So gray and smooth it looked like glass that would cut you just for looking at it. Sometimes it looked still and treacherous, yet at others windblown and whitecapped. Gazing at it chilled me to the bone. But here I am daydreaming.

There is a storm outside. I can see it through the airplane windows.

I am on a very nice private jet that Target sent to take me to do a show for them in Minneapolis. We are traveling at Mach .9, which is the closest to breaking the sound barrier a private aircraft can go, or some such thing. It's all very surreal. No one back home would believe it.

From the cockpit, the captain just informed me that we are eight miles above Colorado. Eight miles! There are flashes of lightning below. He has dimmed the cabin lights so I can better see the explosion of lights burst upward through the dense layers of black clouds, lighting up the night sky and all the stars.

From the ground the storm must be fierce and hard, but from up here it is a silent light show that erupts and dances as if it were performing for me alone.

Vaporous fingers of color begin to fan out on the horizon. Northern Lights! Way up here! I had no idea they had Northern Lights anywhere but in Alaska. For a minute it feels like I'm home, except I'm not staring out the window of a log cabin. I'm in a private plane traveling nearly the speed of sound somewhere high above the Rockies, on my way to sing one song before being whisked off again to the premiere of my first movie, *Ride with the Devil*, at the Toronto Film Festival.

This is different than I expected. It's not like savoring the simple pleasure of guiding a horse silently through the snow-padded fields back home. But I know now that the same awesome force that makes it possible for me to sail the night sky and witness such splendors as tonight ensures that I can return to the splendor of simplicity. And home.

It's all here. Always. Everywhere.

～

Country Hotel Outside of Liverpool

A bowl of bright fruit sits upon what I assume to be an antique table. Not that I'd know a true antique from a reproduction. Where I'm from it's hard to find anything more than, say, fifty years old. Unless you count the only true antiquities . . . the glaciers, mountains, and rugged valleys.

Europe has been mind-boggling. This continent has been inhabited by a modern civilization for centuries. One hundred years ago Alaska was home only to different tribes: Athabascan, Aleut, Tlinket; and perhaps the occasional pillaging explorer.

When I was young, like many in Alaska, I erroneously believed that all of Alaska's natives are Eskimo. But that's like saying all American Indians are Cherokee. There are many proud and distinct tribes—all over Alaska.

When I was seven, I went on tour with my parents to several villages in the Northern interior. I remember flying in bumpy, single-engine planes low over frozen tundra, landing near a cluster of small buildings. I vividly recall being taken by dogsled to the cabin of the family that would be our host for that evening in that village. The dogs—blue-eyed huskies—were excited and yipping, their pink tongues steaming in the cold. They would drown you in licks if you let them.

The ride across a lake to the cabin was endlessly white, giving me the impression that no distance at all was being gained. Though the huskies churned through the snow and the wind bit my face, all I saw was the same pale blur of snow-covered lake, lit by the full moon, and the occasional clutch of scrubby, tough little willow trees. Finally we arrived at a sturdy log cabin. Not the kind of faux-rustic cabin you see in magazines, but the handmade, hand-carved, dark-oiled kind built to endure a hell of a storm.

The woodstove inside warmed the interior abundantly. Suddenly I was peeling off layers of clothing and orienting myself to my new environs. Since it was late, we settled down, ate, and before I knew it, I was asleep. The next morning, I woke in a tall bed covered with a thick homemade goosedown quilt. A new fire had been laid. Still, my nose and ears were cold, as they had been the only body parts that dared to peep out from beneath the thick covers, and I was certainly in no hurry to expose any more skin to the biting air.

Although I remember a great deal about the house, the food, and the resident chickens, dogs, and pigs, I can tell you precious little about our hosts. I remember they were white. The man had a beard and jeans with faded knees and red suspenders. The woman had braided hair and rosy, windburned cheeks. I think they were volunteer schoolteachers in the village. Whatever their other talents may have been, they served up some thick, home-cured bacon for breakfast that was salty and good. Then they harnessed the huskies and whisked us across the frozen lake again to the village.

Out here, far beyond the rim of the urban melting pot, I had expected to find a traditional, native village. I was surprised to discover that the village was made of rough, dirty-looking plywood. The stores, the houses . . . everything. It seemed confusing to me and sad. It looked so poor.

While my dad set up the sound equipment for the gig, my mother and I headed off to change into our show costumes. My hair was strawberry blond and, since I kept it in braids while I slept, long and wavy. Many of the natives had never seen blond hair before, so I was quite a novelty. Sometimes kids would sneak up behind me just to pet my hair. I didn't know what was going on and it scared me until my mother explained.

The gymnasium filled up quickly, and before we knew it, our show was under way. No matter which direction the show took, I could be sure it would have the same finale: a yodeling contest between an audience member and my dad and me—with some sort of small prize awarded to the winner. Back in Anchorage the prize for outyodeling us was routinely a bottle of wine, but many of the more remote villages were "dry." Alcoholism had ravaged several villages. To save their culture and lives, the people in some areas opted to prohibit the sale and consumption of alcohol. So our prize was a bottle of imported sparkling apple cider. At first, when we held it out to the winner, he went pale with excitement and fear, and there was a gasp in the crowd—until my father grinned and announced that the bottle's contents were, indeed, alcohol-free. At another performance, later in the tour, one winner told my mother he was afraid we were going to start a riot.

That evening, the elders invited us to a special dance and ceremony. They wanted to perform for us as thanks for performing for them. I will never forget the hypnotic rhythm of the sealskin drums, the ancient chanting of the singers, the smooth movements and hand gestures of the dancers, who, like the indigenous dancers of the South Seas, told detailed stories about animals and legends and hunts with the subtle movements of their bodies. Best of all, I was given a tight handmade drum to play along with the others. I did everything I could to play evenly and in time. Finally, the elders pulled us up to dance with them as payback for the yodeling. I was shy and terrified, yet I loved it. I swooned like salmon and stamped like caribou. I wasn't just doing it—I was feeling it.

That night we slept in the home of the tribal chief. His daughter let me try on her parka, an incredibly beautiful and practical garment with a soft, badger lining on the inside and durable fabric on the face. I was given gifts, including several scarves and a little drawing. After a hearty dinner, the chief's wife asked if I would like to try some Eskimo ice cream for dessert. Of course I said I would.

"Are you sure?" she asked me.

I got the feeling I was being baited but I said yes anyway. My feeling was confirmed when I was served a big bowl of frozen berries drenched in seal oil and sugar. I ate it stubbornly. The oil was thick and covered my mouth and teeth in a stiff coat of cold, fishy grease. Although many natives today replace the seal oil with vegetable oil, it's still a pretty rugged way to top off a meal.

All in all, my parents and I toured ten or twelve villages during our three-week winter tour. Then we took a small plane back to our orange station wagon and drove the eight hours back home. In the car I felt closer to my parents than ever, honored that they let me sing with them. The experience changed the way I viewed performing. In Anchorage, when we performed at the hotels for tourists, there was no reciprocity, whereas when we sang in the villages, there was a ceremonial exchange of music and craft. The villagers would perform for us and gift us with pieces of handmade art. The sacredness of performing was, for the first time, made obvious to me. It made me feel that it was an honor to sing for others—one worth working hard for.

On the long drive home I worked on mastering my first round, a tune called "Rose Red." A round is a fairly simple song. But if it is sung correctly, and each of the singers begins the melody at exactly the right time, beautiful harmonies result. I practiced the whole way, training my ear for the precise moment when my voice was to enter the tune, the way my friends and I waited our turn to jump into the rhythm of a twirling rope. My parents patiently sang the song over and over. Meanwhile, I yipped and sang like one of those husky puppies, excited by the unforgettable experiences we had just shared, excited to imagine where the adventure of music might lead us next.

~

2:30 A.M.

I lie in the back of my tour bus as we drive from Boston to D.C. It is

2:30 A.M. and everything is upside down. If you took my life as a child and put it to a mirror so that its reflection was the exact opposite, it would be what my life is now.

Air is water. Earth is sky. Quiet is applause. Stillness is perpetual movement. Solace is fame. Open space is a square hotel room and bodyguards at venues. Horse riding is touring in a bus. Mountain air is cigarette smoke. Journal writings have become highly public commodities. Or ingredients for singles. Green fields are now sudden stretches of freeway. Poverty is wealth. Fresh milled wheat and groceries grown by our own hands are now BBQ ribs and McFlurries at convenient stops. Blue sky is something I see on my way from a car to a venue to a bus to a hotel. Playing empty bars has become headlining huge arenas. Private romance has become public fodder.

And here I am doing it, being here, looking in the mirror in the back of the bus, reflecting on who I am. Do I like the dream I've dreamed or have I begun to feel like a prisoner of the dream?

Melbourne, Australia

The lights go down in the house, the music fades, and I walk out to my guitar in the darkness. Nobody knows I'm here until, still wrapped in darkness, I begin to sing the first verse of "Near You Always" a cappella. To hear an entire stadium full of people explode into applause and feel it crash upon me like a wave in the darkness is an experience that inspires an altered state of awareness. Onstage I give in to a flow that is larger than myself. I surrender totally, as I would to the exquisite danger of a silver ice floe, or the overwhelming energy of a deep, silent forest.

In this zone, I am half in supreme control and half in complete obeisance to a thousand signals and sensations. The actual performance sets in motion the balancing of the two. While I definitely guide the show, where it goes is dependent on many variables. Being able to read these variables and remain flexible is part of giving a good performance.

One variable is the crowd. Some artists do the same show every night, regardless of the crowd. Their performances are choreographed right down to the precise word in the exact song when they will drop "spontaneously" to one knee to really sell it. This makes it easier for the light and sound crew and maybe for the performer, but I find it stifling. Each audience has its own zeitgeist—its own mood—that is shared and experienced as a group. Because each show is reciprocal, I'm constantly feeling the crowd to get a sense of what they're into as the night progresses. Some nights people are restless and want to rock. Other nights people are mellow and want only to hear ballads and love songs. Some crowds just got off work, so I avoid my more lyric-driven stuff. Other crowds want their hearts broken. Performing is most satisfying for me when I can tune in to a crowd well enough to know when they are near a breaking point, near crying or near screaming, then picking the moment when we can all push it over the edge. It is a tension that is divine—hopefully for them and certainly for me.

But when everything is on a groove, when I know that a crowd and I are building something together, I can just sit back and lean into a song, feeling my voice gather deep within me, the wind building in my lungs . . . knowing that even before each note fully materializes in my mind it is miraculously and instantaneously married at the vocal cords, given wings, and launched from my very soul. I'd love to take credit for that, but these are sounds that come from beyond myself.

For me, the real beauty of singing is learning to play the instrument I have been given. Each night my voice is different. Like a reed, sometimes it mellows my emotions, rounding their edges until they are smooth as cream. Like a brass instrument, some nights my voice calls clear and crisp; other times it is raspy and strong. My voice is the teacher that instructs me about itself—and, ultimately, about me. I am constantly learning how restraint and control can unlock its depths. But when I just play with it, when I allow it to play me, it is a freedom like no other, like a bird coasting the drafts high in the sky.

∼

In the Midwest

Tonight there was a man wearing a canary yellow shirt sitting in the second row. He was a man who had a history of mental illness and had been convicted of sexual assault, among other things. Word was sent to me backstage that three police officers—one in uniform and two undercover—paid him a visit in his seat, made sure he had no weapons, then left him to enjoy the show.

The whole night I tried not to look to the front left so he wouldn't think I was singing my heart out to him. The show went fine. Though I heard a man talking/yelling oddly during one song and I wondered if it was him. I couldn't really make out what the man was saying because of the earpieces I wear. But my face flushed and I started sweating anyway.

I've slept until 2 P.M. for the last three days. There is so much to dream about.

Bristol

Wake up restless at noon. It is raining and there is a British flag outside my window. It is heavy and limp with rain and twitches like a dying animal in the stiff breeze. A yellow piece of paper has been slipped discreetly beneath my door. It reminds me that I am in Bristol and will be receiving forty calls starting in ten minutes from radio stations across Europe.

My ears are still plugged. They have been since the flight from Japan. Which reminds me of a dream I had last night. Or was it the night before last? A woman came to me and told me my ears were plugged because I feel my whole life has been pulled from under my feet, causing me to feel unstable. I guess my ears symbolize my emotional equilibrium? Doesn't take an analyst for that one. I guess my subconscious decided to give me a break and spell it out for me, rather than hint in rhymes and symbols. Good.

This morning, I woke myself up talking. As I opened my eyes I was saying, "I used to know open fields." Not a new theme, but my voice seemed so small and sad when I said it that it haunts me now. I've always been able to get home at least once a year, no matter how busy. But not this year. There is just no time. I feel lost. I feel small in my life.

This morning I long to open the door and look out upon fields, silver with dew, go catch my horse in the sea mist of early morning, and ride until I outrun every dark mood. That's what I used to do. But when I open the door here, there is only a hallway with a stained carpet and an elevator directly adjacent. The town outside the window is blanketed in thick gray clouds. And although beyond the tangled little city spreads a neat quilt of even, tidy green fields bordered by groomed hedges and stone walls, nothing seems wild here. It is storybook nature. Woods without a wolf.

❦

When I was sixteen, I moved out on my own into the old Bartman cabin, next door to my cousin Arlyn. My cabin was a small, square, one-room affair with no heat beyond what radiated from the small coal stove, which I also used for cooking. There was no running water, either—just a sink that had been set into the counter with a bucket underneath to catch any outflow. Since it was summer and light almost all the time, illumination was rarely an issue. Still, there was one dim lightbulb hanging in the center of the room, perhaps for ambience. In the far corner of the room there was a bed, which had been built from small spruce logs. It was set into the wall, about four feet off the ground. Underneath was "storage space." The only other amenity was a plywood table and one fold-up chair along one wall. Everything in the room—the counters, the stove, the table, the bed—was so close, it was all nearly touching. But I loved it. It was mine. My first home. For the first time in my life, there was no sharing with my brothers. And no one telling me when to do anything, especially to clean.

Living on my own had been my mother Nedra's idea. She and I had been living together in Seward during the school year, and as the last term ended, I became anxious about where to settle. I knew I couldn't live in Homer. My dad had moved into a very small shack while he was building a house, so there was hardly room for me. When Nedra suggested, "Hey—why don't you just get your own place?" it was like the whole world opened up to me. I was an adult! I was trusted! I could live on my own—what a great idea! But how? Would I be okay? And if I could somehow manage to live on my own, could I also make the dreams I held for the next year come true?

My dreams didn't seem easy to fulfill. I felt stuck in Alaska. I suspected that there could be more to life than just being shuffled around from place to place. I had heard about a private school, Interlochen Arts Academy, in Michigan, from a boy in town who had gone there on a dance scholarship. After learning what the school had to offer me—a structure for my music and time to develop my creativity—I told Nedra that Interlochen was the place I wanted to go. But how? I might have been rich in ideas, but money was scarce.

I had just moved into the cabin when Nedra taught me one of the most useful skills I ever learned: how to "manifest dreams." It was like being let in on an alchemist's secret. First, she told me to write down my goal—to make it concrete, if only on paper. Then she showed me how to break it down into daily tasks in order to achieve it.

That's just what I did. First I decided how I would earn the tuition money—by doing a benefit concert for myself. Then, on a piece of paper, I listed the days leading up to the concert and penciled in an assignment for each day. One day, for instance, I would work on posters; another day I would petition some of the people in town for donated prizes I could auction off during intermission. Since Nedra suggested that I work with two adults other than herself, I asked my aunt Sharon and Linda, a family friend, to help with the bookkeeping, the artwork for the flyers, and collections. Finally, I applied for a scholarship and took on a second job working for a local cowboy, giving scenic rides to tourists.

It was a fantastic summer. My cabin was very far out of town. I didn't have a car and hitchhiking in such a remote spot was pointless late at night. Sometimes I wouldn't make it home for two or three days at a time. More often than not, I'd end up camping at friends' places so I could get an early jump on my work in the morning. Some days I'd ride my horse into town, tie him in a friend's field while I worked, then ride the two hours home.

In the end, I got a $13,000 scholarship, and between the concert, the auction, and outright donations, I made just enough money that summer to enroll in Interlochen in September. Most important, I came away with an intimate sense of the strength of my own desire. And of the town's. All of Homer had pulled together to support my dream.

It's all become a cartoon:

GIRL RAISED BY WOLVES IN ALASKAN MUD HUT MOVES INTO CAR, ROCKETS OVERNIGHT TO FREAKISH STAR STATUS!

Stockholm, Sweden, February 1999

Outside the canals are weeping, rising silently above their cement banks. Soundlessly, they spill onto the sidewalk, like a frayed edge. The ground will freeze soon. The night is cold. I can feel it reach my skin through the glass of my window. My pane. My lamp. My towels. Funny how every hotel room becomes my own. My home. If only for one night.

The moon is half-empty . . . on the wane. I feel empty as well. Everything seems melancholy in the light of a moon that is emptying its essence into the greedy darkness.

I can't sleep. It is nearly four A.M. The sun won't rise for some time this far north, this deep in winter. It's like Alaska that way. But different. I draw on myself idly as I lie in bed with my ink pen. Small, flowery, viney wreaths encircle my navel. I become interested and dig a red felt pen from my backpack and color in the roses. I write words around them.

My garden. My springtime. Me.

I come from a very talented gene pool. I recognize that I am merely one link of a chain that has been evolving for generations, as we all are, and that lightning struck my link for some reason. I'm not necessarily the most talented. My kin are uniquely gifted. My paternal grandma was an opera student and poet and the first female Alaskan journalist to write her own award-winning nationally recognized column. My paternal

grandfather was truly one-of-a-kind. A scholar who spoke eight lan-
guages and dialects of each, he distinguished himself as an athlete,
pioneer, cultural researcher, outdoorsman, politician, and "people col-
lector." My aunts and uncles were all raised under their creative
tutelage. For a number of years, my father was home-schooled with his
siblings. Together they learned to speak two languages, play the guitar
and flute, and write creatively. They all wrote songs and plays and
acted and danced and carved.

But for all my grandfather's charisma, charm, and intelligence, he
could be a mean-spirited, hard man, especially to those closest to him.

When I was a kid hitchhiking around Homer, I'd barely get the car
door closed before the driver would ask me, "Are you a Kilcher?" (The
shape of my nose and my high cheekbones are a dead giveaway.)

"Yes."

"Is Yule your grandfather?"

"Uh-huh."

"Man, if I could spend the rest of my days speaking to just one man,
it would be him."

The driver would have made a good choice. Yule Kilcher was not
only brilliant, he was entertaining. He pulled story after amazing story
out of his encyclopedic memory. He could converse with ease about
politics, horseflesh, or the origins of obscure languages. People came
from all over the world to play chess against him. He was very charis-
matic and entertained anyone who came near, captivating them with
his wit and exuberance and rustic manly ways.

I loved my grandpa dearly. He was a man whose respect you wanted
to earn. He could be tender and charming beyond belief, but he was ex-
acting and cruel if you fell out of his favor, which was inevitable if you
spent any time with him. He said I looked like his mother and he had a
soft spot for me. But my unconditional love and respect for him have
never made me blind to his meanness, nor did it make me love him
less. Sometimes I wondered how he could treat others so callously. In
his waning years, he came to regret much of his behavior. Near the end
of his life, he was able to make amends with my father. One day in his
hospital room, Yule took my father's hand and held it more tenderly
than he ever had. He said, his voice full of regret and revelation, "It's all
about love. There just needs to be more love."

I know few details about my grandpa's childhood, but I know it was heavy-handed, as so many childhoods were on old-world farms in the early 1900s. To my grandfather, his eight kids were his property and he worked them very hard—as hard as was needed to clear and homestead land, to grow food, and to bring hay in by hand.

Yule was emotionally and physically abusive to his family. Aside from the physical abuse, he was impatient and a perfectionist. By the time his wife, Ruth, had given birth to her eighth child, she decided to finally leave the new land, and Yule, taking the youngest with her. She was loved dearly by her children, and my father was very close to her. Her departure hurt him—a hurt he would carry into marriage along with his father's legacy.

Of course my father swore he'd never be like his old man, but to break lifelong patterns requires a lot of focus, insight, and time to reflect and renounce old emotional habits. If you never stop and take the time, if you are too busy getting by to initiate change, change will be impossible—no matter how much you want things to be different. My dad went straight from childhood to being drafted to Vietnam; then, on his return, right into marriage at age twenty-two. And before he could begin to resolve the problems of his childhood, he was the father of children of his own.

~

My grandfather traveled all over Europe lecturing on his experiences as an Alaskan pioneer and politician. He was then a state senator. When he was traveling abroad, he'd invite anyone who seemed interested to come and visit him in Alaska. Many did. Often I'd come down the stairs to find a stranger asleep on the couch, a Swiss lady whipping something up on the stove, or a French traveler seated at the table, reading a book. These visitors were an education for me. They told me their life stories, explained about their countries, demonstrated their talents, and gave me books. Almost without exception the visitors were enjoyable, but there was the occasional oddity.

One morning I came downstairs to find a grubby man in threadbare clothing lying on the wood floor with a ragged brown blanket thrown across his torso. Next to him lay a short-haired, chocolate-colored bitch that was sleeping with her belly toward him. I peered at the pair silently from the stairs, trying to figure out what kind of a person this stranger might be, when I noticed he was fondling his dog's teat in his sleep. I raced back upstairs and insisted that my brother Shane go downstairs first.

During the summer, there were adventure/wildlife survival courses that used our homestead as a home base. Consequently there were often large groups of twenty- to thirty-year-olds camped out in tents in our lower fields. Because my mom was not always around, my dad wanted me to have contact with other adults, especially women. He encouraged me to interact with the many types of people who made our homestead their temporary home. I collected their stories the way other kids collected insects . . . from Maine, Italy, Ohio, Argentina . . .

The constant supply of visitors was a gift from Yule that I appreciated at the time and have continued to value more every year since. Contact with so many types of people not only opened the world to me then, but opened my mind to the many types of people I've met since.

❧

New York, Early Spring

Call girls with their hair piled up to ridiculous heights in winding staircases of curls. Bosoms pushed titillatingly high. Tight plastic faux-snakeskin tops that show off the "bald-headed twins" and plenty of midriff. They walk into the suite and mingle with those most likely to be interested. Musicians are a predictable lot.

I am fascinated by these three girls. I ask one the origin of her accent. Lithuania, she tells me. Her hair is platinum and her eyebrows are dark brown. Big brown eyes. Lips turned up at the corners. She seems like a nice girl. All three of them do. Could I have ended up a call girl if nothing else had worked out?

I spent some time with call girls when I was eighteen and living in my car. I had a friend who let me use his shower whenever I wanted. He gave me a key to his place. He worked in a photo lab, developing high-definition black-and-white film. On the side he ran an escort service. It wasn't really upscale stuff, but it wasn't what you'd call low end, either. It was a business staffed by ordinary people.

The girls hung out at my friend's place while they waited for a call. If I happened to be there when they were, we'd talk. I remember one girl who spent three days lying on the couch recovering from a boob job. She was a plump blonde with the palest blue eyes and lips like rose petals that had given up their color. Her chest was so tightly wrapped in bandages it was an effort for her to talk, but she did—if only to tell me she felt like a tractor was parked on her chest. Once the girls asked if I ever thought about dancing in clubs. They knew I needed cash. I said it was a good idea but I didn't think dancing was for me. They never judged me. And I didn't judge them. The truth was that, on the surface, we had a lot in common. I lived in a car and a lot of them had done that, too. We were all doing what we needed to do to get by, hoping something better would come along.

There was no laundry service at my hotel in Glasgow, so the maids took my duvet cover home with them and washed it for me. They returned it white and soft, smelling of normalcy. It smells like their home. It makes me happy to lie on it.

Keep out the night and all its stars they feel so cold

····· with out you ·····

I can understand how Elvis and Judy Garland and countless other performers got addicted to sleeping pills. As the weeks add up on the road, it becomes increasingly difficult to sleep. It takes hours to come down from the buzz I feel after a show. And all of this is complicated by the desire to have a life of my own when I get off a gig, just to watch TV or make phone calls or write.

While it may seem glamorous, virtually every day on the road is taken up, not with museums or parties, as people think, but with work. From dawn to near dawn again is spent on promotion, performance, or travel. Consequently, for me, life begins at night. That's when I can finally kick back and watch movies, catch up on world events, write, draw . . . be. And because I can create or express little of myself during the day in the company of media people, the dead of night is the only time I can write or talk to those people who know me best, as the person I am . . . no more, no less.

Sometimes, the post-gig energy runs so high I dance around my room, playful and wild, like a nocturnal animal. Other times, I just lie on the bed and stare at the ceiling, letting my mind wander. It is often four A.M. before I force myself to sleep. Then, at seven or eight, it's time to wake up, get on the bus, and move on down the road, whether to the next interview or the next country. And before I know it, the whole cycle begins again. Elvis doesn't have to come back from the dead to tell me that this is where sleeping pills begin to look like an attractive option. But not for me.

The cumulative effects of sleep deprivation are hard to cope with. My internal clock is so messed up that I couldn't get to sleep at midnight now if I tried. The road starts to really wear on my health. My mind gets fatigued, making me susceptible to worries and neuroses that usually don't haunt me when I'm rested. The endless hotel rooms start to seem even more stale and cold and unfriendly, always smelling like other people and never like my home. Worst of all, the things that most enlighten my life—like writing or reading—can happen only after it's dark, after everything else has been done. It is ironic and frustrating that writing fuels my career, yet it is now apportioned the least amount of time.

But touring is becoming easier now. I am getting what I need to survive a life on the road. First, I feel my shows are evolving. This satisfies me deeply because it tells me I am still thinking creatively about my craft, learning how to be better at what I do. Most of all, I'm no longer lonely and isolated when I tour because I have a family on the road: my band and crew. Instead of letting me stay in my room, where I can wallow in introspection, they pull me out of the hotel to see a movie, cruise the nightspots, or just pal around. If music is my home, then they are my siblings within that home. And I love them for it.

❧

Tokyo to Osaka

The countryside of Japan flies by the window of the bullet train. The same rocky, misty hills that I have seen in endless paintings of the Orient. Small patches of earth groomed into neat squares that produce the pale faces of cabbages from the dry soil. There are ravens in the cherry trees. The large black birds sit like omens, feathers shiny, amid the virgin white-and-pink blossoms. The image strikes my heart like a fist. Somewhere there must be the fat spotted ponies that I have seen in Japanese paintings, grazing lazily near a stream. Nothing here looks familiar.

Still, I feel peaceful. My drummer has fallen asleep on my shoulder. My two guitarists read magazines and listen to music in the seats ahead of me. U.D. and Felix sit across from us, staring out the window and picking at the pickled contents of the mysterious "lunch box" they purchased on the train. Did Brady remember to eat? Does Doug have enough cash to call his son back home?

I snuggle against the back of the seat. The ultimate luxury may be having others to care about and a song to sing.

＿＿

There is this breath
I hear it everywhere
filling each lung
with a single voice
    more than the meadows,
    more than what is shown,
    more than possessions,
    this is my home
        this voice is my home.

＿＿

At times I feel I am standing absolutely still, flying in so many jets, overhearing so many conversations, seeing the blinding light of children, falling in and out of love, singing for so many faces that peer back at me, wearing my own. Sometimes life is so noisy I feel I will split myself. The motoring sound of a library filled with minds bent on various topics. The symphony of an empty leafless park in New York where dogs wander leashless like old men whose children have forgotten them. And, as I lie down, the missing note of an absent love haunts me like an empty sleeve alive with phantom feeling.

At times I feel I might choke on life. It can seem thoughtlessly cruel and perfectly beautiful. Glorious and painful and precise in its random order. But when I sing, somehow it all begins to make sense. In those smoky barrooms where men dance gallantly and desperately, holding the pale faces of tolerant, abandoned women tightly to their chests; where darts find their way farther and farther from the black bull's-eye of cork dartboards, amid the animated conversation and reverent attention of a few ardent patrons who embrace their drinks with loose abandon, something begins to seem beautiful.

When I sing, order pours out of me, a round warmth that rolls and plays like a bird high on invisible currents, showing me a connection between all things. A sweetness comes over me. People no longer look like car crashes. Singing harmonizes me, uplifts me, shifts my perception. When I sing, I feel divinely whole, like a child who is always dear and loved unconditionally with a vast and all-encompassing love, loved and allowed the grace to make mistakes, loved even when I know my actions to be anything but noble.

When I sing I know somehow in the deepest parts of me that we are all just learning, fumbling toward ecstasy in perpetual youth, gathering experience and runny noses and love poems and tender words and scraped knees like a handful of bright threads, which we weave into our very souls.

When I sing, events don't seem random. When I close my eyes, I can hear beneath the noise of time a mellow hum, the Buddhist Om, the hummingbird's wings, the noise of space and all its stars. My hands do not feel too small and I am cradled and swayed by the voluptuous beauty of all things. Knowing I am part of the rhythm.

This is why I sing.

Even now, when I
grow frightened
or unsure, I hum.

CHAPTER *2*

*I*n sixth grade I chose John to have a crush on. He had long hair, wore only black, and could stick fifteen pins and needles into the back of his hand, then bristle them like a porcupine's quills as he fanned his fingers.

You can see how a girl just couldn't help herself . . .

The beach was quiet and remote. It was not sand, it was rock. Rocks of palm size and larger. Not too comfortable to sleep on. No chance of darkness, either. It was July and the sun just wouldn't go down, even though it was four A.M.

It was my fourteenth summer. I was with my dad and our band in Wasilla to play a gig at a bar called 4 Corners, some four hundred miles from my hometown. We sang country tunes and rockabilly and my dad's originals. Then, after the show, at about one o'clock, we went to another bar to listen to a band called Gary Sloan and the Blues Machine. The bar was crowded and hopping with people busy forgetting the long winter they'd just finished and the things they had to do to prepare for the next one. Alaskans are very live-for-the-moment, seize-life kind of people. Work hard, play hard, never sleep . . . at least, not in the summer.

We sat at a table near the band. People-watching. Suddenly my dad turned to me and nodded toward a guy standing nearby. "See that man over there?" I looked up just in time to see the man saunter past me. "He's going to ask that lady over there to dance with him," he informed me.

I looked over at the end of the room. Sure enough, there was a lady standing alone at the bar. "Remember this, Jewel," my dad said. "The long walk up to a woman, with all eyes watching, is one of the longest walks in a man's life. If she accepts, it's okay—but the walk back alone? Well, that's the longest walk of all."

Through the smoke, I focused on the twosome at the bar. The exchange was brief. The lady had obviously declined. For a second the man seemed to hide under his hat, then he puffed himself up a bit and walked self-consciously back to his buddies.

"You can tell a lot about a man by the way he makes that return trip," my dad continued. "It takes a very confident man not to be embarrassed or defensive. A lot of girls will change their minds and dance with you later in the evening if you're okay with the letdown. If you get all weird, it's a turnoff."

By now, my dad was doing a fairly decent Howard Cosell imitation, a complete play-by-play of the interaction between the men and women at the bar. I found it endlessly amusing. *The pitch, the windup—oh! Swing and a miss!*

In the course of that night, Dad took the long walk a few times himself, but saved a couple of dances for me. It was nearly four A.M. before we began pitching our tent on the windy rock beach. We crawled into our sleeping bags, packed inside the tent like sardines: my dad, the drummer, the keyboard player, the guitarist, and me.

I went to sleep tired and happy, hardly aware of the midnight sun still glowing on the horizon.

What do you learn about sex in barrooms? You learn that some people are willing to trade their dignity for a little attention. You learn that sometimes a job interview includes a "screw test." You learn that even if a woman agrees to take the screw test, she might not get the job. Just the screw. If you're lucky, like me, you learn all this from others' experience when you're still too young for sex but old enough to observe and remember the stories.

San Francisco

Tonight a boy was crying in the crowd. But not a boy. I think he was in his mid to late twenties. His eyes were red and his cheeks were smeared and wet. Then, between "You Were Meant for Me" and "Life Uncommon," he yelled at me miserably, "You sellout. You sellout." He looked at me with sincere disappointment, like Achilles having just realized his one weakness.

"I'm a sellout?" I said it back into the mike. He looked back at me pitifully. I did what I could to recover and come up with some light banter, but I couldn't help but consider his accusation. What had I done? What did he mean? I launched into the next song, but while I was singing I wondered what I could possibly have done to disappoint a total stranger so completely. Some commercial? The movie? Too much rock material and not enough folk?

Then some girl yelled, "Kick his ass, Jewel!" This was no consolation. Could he have been the same guy who threw the Mardi Gras beads at me? When I started the show someone threw a necklace to me on-stage. It hit me in the face, so I threw it back in the general direction it came from. Everyone cheered but the person who threw it, I suppose. Maybe it was that boy.

Later I noticed that a security guard was messing with him. He wasn't reacting, just crying still. Security was telling him to get back. I stopped in the middle of "Foolish Games" and told the guards he was okay and to leave him alone. But he ended up leaving anyway, his body crumpled and defeated and limp.

I want love to be simple. I want to trust without thinking. I want to be generous with my affection and patience and love unconditionally. It is easier to love a person with their flaws than to weed through them. I want to love the whole person, not parts; and this is how I want to be loved.

After the Phone Call, 4:30 A.M.

He wants a long song. He wants a fairy tale, for pearls to fall from my lips and awaken in him the things he has forgotten. He wants more than my words, more than my kisses, more than the possession of my body. He wants the parts of me I save for myself—that I cannot give away. The craggy peaks and unfathomable depths of imagination that form the to-pography of my inner world, which is boundless and untamed and belongs to no one. To give that mystery to anyone would be to destroy the very essence from which all other things about me radiate, like the endless rings that emanate from a single stone dropped into still waters.

But still I lay what I can at his feet. What I give to him is delicate. Cuticle . . . the tender translucent nebula, which would cause me to bleed if the delicate edges frayed. I have tried. I have given to the point of feeling empty, but he is still not full. There is not enough love in me. I am too small. He needs a greater love—the love of God—but he is afraid of God and hungry for answers I cannot possibly give. And he is angry, angry with more than me.

He shakes my shoulders, demanding more. And I, like a foolish child, do not leave but try to give more. It helps no one.

⸙

Gary Dwight was not terribly nice to me. Really, he had no reason to be. I was a shy seventh-grader who overcompensated by being awkwardly outgoing and touchy. Maybe he was a shy kid as well, who overcompensated by giving me snide looks and teasing the other kids who rode in the back of the bus on the way home from school.

None of that mattered, though. To me he was dark and handsome and dangerous. He was a ninth-grader. Needless to say, I had an enormous, debilitating crush on him. All I could do was barely think of some acceptably smart comeback when he'd turn his big, brown, dark-lashed eyes toward me and spew something full of venom in my direction.

Really, he didn't know I was alive. I was just another of the many flat-chested junior-high kids who pestered him and hung around. But one summer day it looked like my luck might change.

I was helping my dad lay a foundation for my grandfather's new basement. We had already jacked up his house, moved it over, and dug a level bottom. Now we were building the foundation up, layer by layer, with cement blocks. The foundation wall was about up to my waist, the sun was hot, and I was scooping wet cement out of a bucket and spreading it neatly onto a block when I heard two three-wheelers roaring down the road. Before I knew it, Gary Dwight himself was parked right in front of us, my brother Shane perched on the seat behind him. I could hardly believe it! My brother . . . friends with the very man who had possessed my every thought for months!

Gary's best friend, Aaron, was on his own ATV parked next to Gary. As Shane hopped off, Aaron asked if they could use our road to go down to the beach. My dad said yes and they sped off, kicking up loose dirt, leaving my dad shaking his head.

Shane picked up a trowel and dug in. "Crazy driver that Gary is," he offered.

"Oh, yeah?" my dad grunted.

"He drove right into the pole gate and cracked a pole," Shane continued.

Dad gave a look that meant, *Well, guess who has to fix it?*

Then silence. That was all I was going to get. I'd just have to wait until they drove back up to go home.

After about forty minutes we heard an engine screaming up the hill. It was Aaron, tearing across the field. He stopped right in front of us, his eyes wide and glassy, like saucers filled with milk. Then he spoke.

"G-Gary went over the edge! He went over the edge of the canyon and he's coughing up blood!"

At first we wondered if it was a prank, but he was too spooked. My dad sprang into action. He yelled for Bo, a ranch hand, to get his Jeep. While Bo pulled up, my dad ran for a phone and called a doctor he heard was staying with someone up the road. Then he jumped into the Jeep and looked at me. "Are you coming?" I climbed in without thinking and off we zoomed at breakneck speed, no one saying a word.

The beach road wandered for a mile through various fields, then, in the last quarter mile, turned winding, treacherous, and steep along the canyon. Apparently it was there, on a turn, that Gary had gone over. Sure enough, Aaron pointed over the edge of the canyon and there he was—up against one of the many alders, the three-wheeler just below.

He looked dead. He definitely wasn't breathing; his eyes were half-open and there was pink bubbly blood coming out of his mouth. We jumped down the steep slope. I grabbed one leg, Aaron the other, and Bo lifted him under each arm. Carefully, as gently as possible, we carried him to the top.

It didn't look good. His body was limp and no movement was returning to his limbs. There was no life in him at all. Bo turned to me and Aaron and said, "Why don't you two walk back. I'll drive Gary up to see if maybe the doctor can . . ." His voice trailed off.

Shock set in on the long walk home. Aaron was rambling and talking and freaked out; the whole ordeal was hitting him like a train. I tried my best to comfort him. I let him talk, told him that it wasn't his fault, and just listened. But we both felt that the whole world had changed. Everything was different. Nothing would ever be the same. How could it? There was one less person in the world! I couldn't accept how final it was—an hour ago, he was there, alive, breathing, and an hour later it was irreversibly and finally the other way. There was no second chance, just one final solemn unthinkable truth that had changed all life forever.

When we came to the barn we saw that Gary had been laid out on a thin strip of grass at the edge of the garden in front of the house. He was covered by a bedsheet. My dad was talking with the doctor, who had walked over from the neighbor's in his flannel shirt and khakis. He looked like a nice enough man. Bushy long beard, small round spectacles, and as helpless as the rest of us.

My dad told us that he had called Gary's parents as soon as it happened. He told them that he wasn't sure how the accident had unfolded but we had gone to help and that they should come over. Now we were just waiting for them to arrive. My dad looked blök. I felt dizzy. I went inside and sat in front of the large window, watching the scene from a distance as if it were happening on a movie screen. Everything was wrong, but the day was sunny and beautiful. The blue sky, the cauliflower blooming, the white sheet on the green grass. It was all like a movie. A man and a woman drove up in a burgundy Subaru. They walked through the gate toward my dad. When the woman saw the sheet that was covering her son, she crumpled like a dry leaf. Her husband fumbled to support her, still in disbelief. The woman hid her face, a primitive keening rising from deep within her. I could hear her from inside the house.

I didn't want to watch anymore. I left the window and sat on the couch. Then I went upstairs to my room. The whole house seemed filled with that woman's grief.

I noticed numbly that the top sheet was missing from my bed.

～

As much as my childhood was shaped by the beauty of the natural world, it was also molded by the painful knowledge of how much people suffer. Even the small

*indignities the human spirit endures
. . . taking crap from petty bosses
just to get a minimum-wage paycheck
. . . answering personal questions
in the welfare office, like whether
you have a boyfriend who gives
you money, just so you can get
your children fed in one of the
richest countries in the world . . .
these are the kinds of things that
inspired me to write songs like "Who
Will Save Your Soul?" at age sixteen.*

Philly, '95

We stopped at a traffic light in Philadelphia. It was another day, another town, another drive in a record rep's car to another radio station so that I might sing for them in hopes they'd do more than offer me another sandwich . . . like actually add my song to the playlist. The window was rolled down and I drooped half out of it, my chin propped up like the head of a wilted flower. A beat-up old Chevette that was some seventies shade of brown pulled up next to me.

The girl driving had the window down and was looking straight ahead. She couldn't have been more than nineteen. I stared at her, admiring the longevity of her beat-up old car, the startling brightness of her simple white cotton shirt against the dingy upholstery. Her hair was shiny, and had been hastily combed into messy pigtails. She must have felt me staring because she looked over at me.

In our separate cars at the red light, our noses couldn't have been more than three feet apart. I must have looked strange to her—a pale and scrawny girl with tired, red eyes, crumpled in the front seat. Her appearance certainly made an impression on me. She had a whopping black eye. Looked like yesterday's affair—still pretty fresh. The whole side of her face was swollen. Someone really put it to her. It was the kind of shiner that took some effort to give.

I wondered if she was on her way back to whoever did it, with the groceries next to her in the seat. I wondered what could make her stay. I wanted to tell her to just keep driving until she got out of Philly—or until she got beyond the reach of the relationship that had wounded her. She had the car . . . she had some gas.

Then what? Getting by in a place you know can be hard enough, especially for a poor young girl. How do you get by in a place you don't know?

The light turned green. We drove side by side up the street, then turned away from each other. Maybe she won't ever go near the person who did that to her. Maybe she just got in a fight with some girl and it wasn't her boyfriend or father or anything like that at all.

⁓

One day, when I was about six, my parents sat us all down and told us they were going to be divorced. We laughed. Not because we thought it was funny but because the idea was so unimaginable to us we were sure it was a joke. And for a while it wasn't that serious. My parents didn't live together, but we had access to both of them. We even continued to perform our summer show together for two seasons after the divorce. But one day my father told us that we'd be moving with him 220 miles away, from Anchorage to Homer. We had a vague sense that it would happen, but we had no way of knowing what it would mean.

It happened finally after our last show together. The station wagon was packed with our belongings. My brothers Atz Lee and Shane and I climbed into the backseat for the all-night drive to Homer.

I looked out the back window. There was my mom, still dressed in her costume—a long denim skirt, a ruffled burgundy shirt, and a hat with a feather in the band. She was waving good-bye to us. As I was waving back, I noticed that the stiff fabric of her skirt was shaking. My mother was sobbing, though her face was trying hard to be cheerful. I stared in shock. The unthinkable was happening. I was being torn out of the soil in which I had grown. Tender roots left to dangle in the raw, unfriendly air. How would we kids sustain ourselves? We were no longer whole.

I remember my brothers and me, stiff in our seats, really wanting to cry, but at the same time not wanting to cry at all. Finally Shane told a joke and we laughed at first but then started to cry uncontrollably.

Our mother was growing smaller in the rearview mirror. We were driving away, away from life as we knew it, toward the uncertainty of our new lives in Homer.

⁓

I was five. In the story my mother tells, she and I were traveling in Utah. She had arranged to meet an old friend in a park near a certain tree. As we pulled into the park, she could see her friend waiting for her.

She said to me, "Just wait here and I'll catch her attention." She started to get out of the car. But before she could really take a step, I grabbed her and said, "No, Mom. Don't leave me."

My mom explained that she had no intention of leaving me. She was just going to stand near the car door and call her friend's name. And she started to do just that when I grabbed her again and said, "Mom, don't leave me." She leaned toward me in the seat and calmed me down. Did I want to get out of the car with her? Would that make me feel better? No, I said.

She stopped then and looked at me. "What is it, Jewel?" she asked quietly.

"Promise me you'll never leave me," I repeated.

"What do you mean?"

"You have to promise," I insisted. "Without you, how will I ever know right from wrong?"

"It won't ever be like that," she said. "I won't ever leave you."

⁓

The divorce snuck up on me. I didn't see it coming. We were Mormons, for heaven's sake! Mormons don't get divorced!

My parents fought a lot. I knew that. They fought behind closed doors, sometimes for hours at a time. But divorce seemed so unthinkable. Had I missed the signs?

After the divorce I became obsessed with scrutinizing my family life for clues and signs that might signal change. Even from a young age, when we were all together, I had kept track of those closest to me and their emotions. But after the divorce I began writing regularly for the first time. I studied the romances that began in the bars I sang in, searching for deeper motivations and hidden sorrows. I watched my dad, trying to predict his moods so they wouldn't catch me off guard.

My need to observe and understand was the beginning of my poetry and, in many ways, this book.

Love . . . this love . . . like the strong and delicate folds of an origami box. It strengthens with each kiss of paper upon paper. And so it is unmade the same way, unfolding day by day, promise by promise—as we unfold ourselves.

How do you deconstruct the house that love built? Corner by corner, vow by vow. Unthinkably alone.

Always find a way to call out of another the highest in themselves.

When I was eighteen and in love for the first time, my boyfriend and I drove from San Francisco to San Diego, then to Colorado, where I would live, in Boulder, for the next few months.

I remember those days as long and lush, filled with sun and junk food and oil checks. We slept in the back of his truck . . . in sheltering groves of trees, on desert plains, on the edge of canyons, amid herds of lazily grazing wild horses.

First love avoids conflict. Young lovers are quick to forgive and forget—perhaps because they love for love's sake . . . or maybe because they are somehow aware that they lack the skills necessary to address problems or change behaviors.

First love is delicious and brutal. It is a bright fire that burns both hearts out. First love is all heart: new, raw emotions, with no rational structure on which to hang them. And it is often blind. First-time lovers cannot see condescension and jealousy for the inadequate defenses they are. They are somehow flattered by overbearing affection and jealous demands. Young love is a reckless adventure of abandon, a complete surrender to the fullness of emotion. And a young lover bathes in this recklessness like a child immersed in the warm, exotic pool of its first holiday.

First love was a wonderful and exhausting time for me. It also felt dangerous, somehow. It was as though some part of me was aware that it was too intoxicating and somehow unreal, like a fantasy. That my whole life had become consumed. And that if I allowed it to continue, I would never know my life's purpose. I would never know myself.

Before I realized it, marriage and kids had become a topic of conversation, though a fanciful one, because discussing such subjects made us feel grown up. And I began to understand, *Hey . . . this is how it happens. This is how I end up too young and married with kids; it's talked about, then it's real.* I was beginning to suspect I wasn't truly in love. I was in love with the idea of being in love.

With time, my deepest cravings became impossible to ignore. Though I cared for him, I longed for my own destiny. And so I explained my feelings to my very surprised boyfriend with the best words I knew—which were, perhaps, not chosen carefully enough—and left, shocked and alone. In a single moment, I had given up the only future I had ever imagined, a future with him, and began to imagine a life of my own. I would begin to discover my passions and dreams.

⌘

When I was young, I enjoyed seducing myself with the possibility of who a boy might be rather than who he actually was . . . avoiding real information.

Boys weren't real. They were the point from which my desire began to create itself.

Gradually I became less interested in invention and more interested in intimacy.

≈

Shortly after the divorce, my brothers and I were enrolled in a class for the children of enlightened parents who wanted to engineer "progressive" divorces. The class was called "Mommy and Daddy Still Love You" or some corny thing like that. The pretty therapist would repeat it often with emphasis and wide, toothy smiles.

It was pitiful, even to us. There we were, among all these broken little kids in their winter jackets, being dropped off by one half of the divorcing couple, then picked up an hour later by the other half. We got through it, though. Mainly because we knew there would be a bag of candy at the end and because, just as with the divorce, we had no choice but to do what our parents decided for us.

What did we learn there? We learned to watch for techniques our parents might use to win our love. Like the "Disneyland technique," where one parent tries to spoil you into preferring him or her. Or the "marital mud sling," where the insecure parent constantly slanders the ex. Of the two, the Disneyland technique was definitely preferable.

My brothers and I also learned something else. How to pick up strange vibes that Mary Lee's father might be more familiar with the therapist than the other fathers seemed to be.

≈

Once my mom was gone, my dad wanted to make sure I had female influence in my life. And I always did.

Dad's "friends" would try to bond with me, the only daughter. I suppose they felt sorry for me somehow, living on a ranch with only men and no modern conveniences. Or maybe they were just looking for a way to get at my dad and saw me as the weak point in the family armor. Whatever the reason, their advances were awkward and embarrassing and feminine in an exaggerated way. "Would you like to play with my purse?" they'd ask me. Or "Hey, I know . . . let's play makeup!!!" (Always plenty of exclamation marks!!! And happy, just-between-us smiles!!!) I guess it was hard for them to imagine I never really felt I was missing out on much—even though I was living on a homestead in the middle of nowhere with no other bipedal females in sight.

Sometimes they'd get very personal. They'd whisper, "Do you wear a bra yet?" or "Are you developing?" I'd just smile and remind them, "I have a mother." They were all nice enough, but their instant familiarity struck me as insincere. My brothers and I tried our best to get on with all of them, but eventually we gave up. After the first few you can't help but become detached.

There was good reason Dad attracted so many women. He was very romantic and creative. He was the kind of man who made women jewelry and wove them beautiful baskets and wrote love songs to serenade his loves on horseback. His dates didn't stand a chance, really. And eventually one of them, Donna, inspired a series of songs and the turnover came to a sudden halt.

We kids knew our dad was up to something. Often our father would spend days on end creating a special gift for a girlfriend. But this time he had been holed up in his room for several weeks, crafting. But what? Whenever we went snooping we found only bits of silver foil, which were no clue at all. We had no choice but to wait.

Finally, on a warm summer evening, we got our answer. Donna arrived just before sunset wearing a long, white cotton dress. Father directed her to wait for him in the second field—a long, downward slope of green grass and swaying timothy with a dazzling view of the icy blue bay and the mountains that bounded it on the other side. Then he confined us to the house, reassuring us he'd come for us soon.

Several hours passed. Unable to contain our curiosity, we burst out of the house and ran to the field. It was empty! We dashed to the "Octagon Cabin," figuring it was the most logically romantic spot.

The Octagon Cabin was just that: a cabin with eight sides, four of which were large glass panels that overlooked what seemed like the whole of the world. It was perched right on a bluff above the shore. We saw Toklat, our large white gelding, tied outside. We'd found them! We shoved open the door and toppled in to find my father sitting stiffly on the floor, wearing a suit of armor he'd made from cardboard and foil. Clearly, the woman with him had been chosen as his princess. There were two glasses of wine between them. And a ring. Suddenly I wasn't so sure I felt like being there anymore.

"I'm glad you kids are here," my dad said, smiling. "I've just asked Donna to marry me . . . and she's accepted."

childhood

Just the three of us—my brother Shane, my pot belly, and me

My grandfather Yule on the homestead in Alaska

My dad's parents and siblings (left to right): Mairiis, Ruth, Wurtila,

Yule, and Fay

Yule holding court at a wedding

Family photo—Mom, Atz Lee, Shane, Dad, and me

Me on garden detail, about age 16, on the site where my dad was building a cabin. This is the spot where he first sang "Sweet 16 Lullaby" to me.

Me giving a neighbor a ride on my horse Clearwater. I was about 14 or 15 here.

These shots were taken on the tour that we made through the northern interior of all the Alaskan native villages.

That's me sitting in the sled on our

way to the cabin we would sleep in.

One of the chief's houses that we stayed in

My dad with an Eskimo woman

A cabin built on stilts, so it won't get buried in snowstorms

My 2nd birthday at the house in Anchorage, Alaska

Fishing in Seward, Alaska

Posing at a fair

First-day-of-

First-day-of- school blues

Me in the showroom of Vitrics, my mom's glass gallery

This picture was taken
by that guy who ended
up being the child
pornographer-molester. He
kept telling me to "pose pretty, be sexy, just like Miss America."
I ended up looking defiant and stubborn.

Another winter on the homestead—

Me getting ready to splat the photographer with a snowball. This is when we had just landed in a native village to sing.

other in June of '00. This cabin is my aunt's, and I practically lived here in the summer. It's at the head of the bay, and we'd sleep here on long cattle drives. These were taken in the same cabin, one on my 11th birthday, the

Brushing Toklat

I used to nap on Enchantress while she grazed with the herd in the fields.

Me and Clearwater

sun. My cousin Dylan took both of these shots.

waking from a nap. I used to sleep curled up to his belly when he lay in the

At 14 I went through a Cole Porter phase. I still love the music of that era, but I have let go of the pillbox hats...

On the edge of McNeil Canyon, which borders the homestead

This is the barn I grew up in.

My dad, Atz

Ty Murray (to my left) and me with the Martushev boys—Akaky, Zahari, and Filip. I grew up riding with these boys (especially Filip) in the flatlands.

This is at the homestead next to the barn—not a bad view for a tree swing.

I don't remember my brothers' reaction but I know we all put on smiles. In my own heart, I wished it was my father alone who was gaining a new wife and not us. It wouldn't be just the two of them getting hitched, after all—it would be all five of us. Plus her little girl. Couldn't she just keep living in her house? Couldn't they find some way to marry each other and keep us out of it?

In the days that followed, I was quiet . . . not sore or resentful, just trying to adjust. Luckily I didn't end up having to change a thing. Donna backed out of the marriage. She said that being swept off her feet by a knight on a white horse, being presented with a ring he had made himself, was dizzyingly romantic. The emotions of the moment went straight to her head, and though she had questions about making the relationship long-term, she just couldn't break the momentum. I guess the momentum was more easily broken a week and a half later.

We kids were relieved. As for my dad, he was disappointed but okay. Maybe he was relieved, too.

My father reacted to the divorce like the social worker he was: with platitudes and advice and therapists' numbers scrawled on the calendar. He was upset but going to "work through it." What I remember about my mother was the crying. Because Nedra had no income, we lived with my father.

Suddenly, everything she knew to be real about her life was turned upside down. It wasn't good enough that she was an artist, a mother, a performer. She needed a steady income or she couldn't have custody of us. I learned early on that money matters—a lot.

I remember thinking that after the divorce she seemed like a turtle that had been flipped onto its back. She appeared so helpless.

She would get back on her feet, this time under her own power.

When I was thirteen, I saw an elderly woman on a plane. She was sensuous and soft and strong, and I was transfixed, not only by her beauty but by the suggestion in her walk that she had come to know the power of both softness and strength.

I was a flat-chested kid the next row over. What did I know? Only this: that this woman had known the hot whispers of a man who loved her, entirely if not eternally. And that she had answered, fiercely soft.

Singapore

It's after the show. I head for my room. My throat is too tired to talk. I can always write. But what? Well, it's my book for now.

A former boyfriend thought that because I was famous it meant I needed attention. He never believed that what I wanted was to be with one man, to make myself small in his arms. Seems fitting, somehow. My insides will be known by strangers, yet I was a stranger to a man who claimed to love me.

I saw you again. You're
still full of shit but
you're better than most.

My fondest memories of my dad are of him and horses. I remember sitting and watching him for hours breaking colts to lead and ride. There he is, forever in my mind's eye, in his jeans and black diamond-stitched cowboy boots . . . and the hat, always the hat: an old beat-up straw number, its brim bent and curled tight to the crown. Very cool.

Like most daughters, I thought my dad was the most handsome and clever man in the world. And I marveled at his many talents—evidence of his greatness. He was quick and strong with horses, but gentle, too. I'd help him in the corral. He'd teach me some of the old tricks. How to tie a colt to the inner tube of a tractor tire so that when the colt reared and pulled, the elastic tube would snap the horse back in, teaching it not to resist. How to rope a colt to its mother's neck, and let the mare teach her baby to lead. He'd teach me to tie knots, teach me to coax a colt gently, getting it to come to me one step at a time, while heeding his reminders to watch that my fingers didn't get caught in the rope's coils.

My dad was great at bucking horses. He could ride 'em till they just gave up. Though I watched him for years, I never saw him get thrown off. As for me, I was so busy figuring out a soft spot to land that I forgot to hang on. I promised Dad to try to remember to stay on, and eventually I started getting the knack of it. But I just didn't have the aura of quiet authority or the ability to communicate to animals that he did.

Dad and I spent long days together riding miles across the Alaskan wilderness. He'd play me his new songs around a campfire or perched on a fence. Like most artists, he shaped his works from what he knew: the land and the rivers and his horses. He played his songs for me on an old guitar that was delightfully out of tune, his voice confident and strong, forging bravely ahead down the unsure path of a new melody. My dad seemed perfect at those moments. Whole and full of himself. Not like the dad who was divorced and living back on the farm where he was raised. Not like the man who was raising two boys and a perplexing daughter. That man, who could barely make ends meet, was locked in tension and worry, living a life that didn't come close to the dream he dreamed as a child.

But watching him rope cattle at dusk, seeing the blue of the sky mirrored in his eyes, I knew that no matter what mysterious sorrow haunted my dad, he had given me all that I needed. He taught me to sing, to work hard, to ride out hardship. And how to tie knots. One day I would learn to untie them.

⮑

My relationship with my father was a challenging one. For reasons that neither he nor I could fathom, he was challenged and felt threatened. He disliked me from my first cry. He was critical and impatient, suspicious and harsh with me. There was a lot of tension, disapproval, and pain. Dad was raised by an abusive father whose own father received a harsh parental legacy as well. Dad's father used to say to him, "It says in the Bible that the sins of the fathers are visited on the children for seven generations, and it's damned true." My father's deepest fear—which he began to act out on his children—was that he would continue the chain of emotional and physical abuse. It was also his deepest vow not to do so.

My early years, and especially those following the divorce, were years of great conflict within him as he struggled to correct ingrained patterns, resolve his confusions about parenting, and learn new methods, as well as heal the considerable wounds of abuse he suffered as a child. Unlike his father, he rarely lost control and hit me; more often he raged and harangued at me emotionally. His disapproval and criticism of me was so intense that eventually I internalized that harsh critic's voice. I came to drive myself mercilessly, seeking an approval from others that I wasn't willing to give myself. I have carried a deep loneliness and sorrow. The confusion and fear from that important relationship led me to be a chronic worrier, to have a high need to control whatever I could, and led me in and out of a number of unfulfilling relationships with boyfriends. Gradually I have come to understand the source and the antidote for these issues. I've learned to ask for help and support, and to receive love. I've grown in self-esteem and confidence, learning to be gentle with myself—less judgmental and mean to myself. I'm learning to open up and be more trusting in relationships. I am feeling whole and far more satisfied with myself, and patient with my shortcomings.

My relationship with my dad was less about nurturing and guidance than about boundaries, acceptance, and struggling toward self-love. It has been a path of pain and, ultimately, victory. He did not give up on this struggle, consistently requiring himself to grow and change. This has been a gift to me in my own healing process. I no longer feel anger or blame, because he has taken responsibility and made amends. We've both learned that people are not irreparably damaged by their experience, that we do grow strong in areas where we were weakened. I was hurt but not damaged. I've had things to work through, and sorrows, but I can say to others who have suffered that we are whole no matter how broken we feel, and we can recover the experience of our wholeness, no matter our age.

When I was sixteen, I moved out on my own into a cabin across the canyon from my dad. Neither of us had telephones. If he wanted me to come over, he would yodel across the canyon. If I yodeled in response it meant I was on my way.

One day, my dad called me over and said he had a song to play me. (Though my dad put out a new CD in 1999 and updated the lyrics, the song he sang to me was nearly the same as the lyrics printed here.)

Sweet Sixteen Lullaby

You turned sixteen today—and you tell me you're movin' away—just a little cabin across the way—on the other side of the canyon—you won't be far from me—not so far that you can't see—should you decide to call on me—you can yodel on the wind—raised in the wilderness Alaskan woods—livin' was hard but the music was good—I know I didn't always do all I should—but we made it through somehow—now they're hearing your music from the White House to Rome—cover of *Time* and *Rolling Stone*—but sometimes you seem so far from home—my little Jewel, I'm proud.

Chorus . . . Time flies, years roll away—Daddy, sing me back to yesterday—I didn't always hear my little girl say sing me a lullaby—but you can't go back again—life has been what life has been—but you'll never be too old for me to sing—a sweet sixteen lullaby—sweet sixteen lullaby—a yodeling lullaby . . . yodel . . .

There's a time to hold on and a time to let go—you've always had a mind of your own—it hasn't always been an easy row to hoe—but you gave it the best you had—late-night talk shows, doin' your thing—I hear you on the radio when you sing—but I love it most when the telephone rings—and I hear you say, "Hi, Daddy . . ."

Chorus . . . Time flies, years roll away—Daddy, sing me back to yesterday—I didn't always hear my little girl say sing me a lullaby—but you can't go back again—life has been what life has been—but you'll never be too old for me to sing—a sweet sixteen lullaby—sweet sixteen lullaby—a yodeling lullaby . . . yodel . . .

My dad and I had not yet spoken of what had passed between us. I couldn't help being touched at the realization that this was my father's poetic way of making amends.

My father was in no way a mean person. He was wounded, and acted out of his wounds, and for the younger years of my life he was almost like a child who was in over his head after the divorce. I think a lot of parents can relate to that. He did not try to act like abuse was acceptable behavior, or our fault, or refuse to let us talk about it. It troubled him deeply about himself and he very bravely and tenaciously set about working on himself. I respect this very much because so often patterns learned in childhood go unbroken. This is very heroic to me, and I am proud of my dad for the man he has become. I am so pleased to go home and see him happy, with his horses and his music and his continuing healing. It is a miracle.

My father and I have discovered what we value in each other, we've learned what to leave alone—we have a past that no longer continues to constantly rise up between us. It makes me very happy that he now respects and enjoys me, and I him. It pleases me to see him satisfied in a new marriage and gently fathering his new family. At times we are still awkward, occasionally we feel like strangers, but we are more comfortable with the gaps and differences between us. I'm proud of our work together and it feels good to know that the unhappy legacy of the previous generations ends with us. When I see my brother Atz with his two-year-old stepson or watch my brother Shane playing patiently with his four children, I know it has.

When I'm on the road and I see the nature of most of the guys I meet, I find myself overlooking any imperfections in the man I'm seeing and feeling quite thankful I've found such a decent chap at all. But I don't suppose that's what they call "true love," is it?

❧

NY to London

I am sitting in British Airways' first-class lounge in the only open seat available, which is, unfortunately, right next to the smoking lounge. As much as I mind smoke, it turns out to be secondary in offensiveness to the conversation that seeps through the glass doors to the area where I am sitting.

"I am Mr. Viagra!" Did I hear that right? I position myself nearer to the doors so that I might see who owns this announcement. It is a businessman in mismatched golf clothing with red hair. You know the type. The kind of man who makes someone like Manuel Noriega look alabaster-complexioned and classically handsome.

"Mr. Viagra" is on his feet, enthusiastically entertaining eight or nine other men who look remarkably like him. He explains to his eager audience that he is somehow connected with the pharmaceutical company that invented the drug. What he does next has my mouth on the floor. He tells his friends about a new service they can call that provides a businessman—or a horny old jerk, as the case may be—with a phony telephone number. This, he says, ensures him that he'll always show up "clean" on his wife's Caller ID so he can call and say "I'm in Chile on business," and really be screwing his girlfriend in Brooklyn! He humps the air aggressively for emphasis.

The men laugh.

The next thing I know, the door of the smoking lounge is thrown open and the man whose voice I have been listening to steps out. He walks past me, looking me up and down lasciviously, winking as he walks. It is too much. I can't help myself.

"Are you 'Mr. Viagra'?" I ask him, swooning like a Dallas Cowboys cheerleader.

He is impressed. He puffs his chest out and raises his bushy eyebrows as if to say, *At last . . . my public recognizes me!* Then he composes himself and answers in a thick, low voice, "Why yes, I am."

By this time he has completely undressed me with his eyes and is preparing to drag me off to someplace he'll call his wife from later to say he is in London. The whole scene is a cartoon in which he has been cast as a caricature of himself.

As calmly as I can, I stand up, look him up and down, and say, "Well, I guess necessity is the mother of all invention."

"Aren't you Jewel?" he asks.

❧

By the River

I awoke this morning to the sound of birds and the smell of pine. I awoke in strong arms. Arms smooth and fine as the chalky bellies of young birch. His arms are tough, his hands are rough and thick and raise hell in the day, but at night they are the most tender extremities, capable of conveying such sweet sentiment that it gives my heart pause.

He kissed me beneath the light of the moon, at the edge of a river. He hovered above me, both our bodies drenched in celestial glow, making our skin translucent. Looking without looking, I could see the clockwork of his soul. I feared he could see the hummingbird that lives in my chest and speaks only in whispers with a tiny voice. So naked did I feel beneath the blue-sky-steady gaze of his eyes that I wanted to retreat inside myself where it was quiet again. Still waters, not messed up by romantic embraces and hot whispers.

Such torrid seas I have been sailing these last years, which, at first, promised calm. It has caused me to doubt my judgment. In my mind grew a shadow that cautioned me to be alone. And so I have been. No man has come close. I have been quiet and withdrawn. No pretty face or handsome jaw or clever turn of phrase or simple flattery lured me out from the deep waters of my soul. So did I feel disappointed I found a man who, when he held me, felt familiar? Perhaps a little. Afraid? Yes, that too, for many reasons. First, because of how sincerely I liked him and a feeling of doom that if we were more than friends I would lose the privilege eventually of knowing him. Second, because my life does not look like it used to and I doubt at times its ability to sustain a relationship. There is so much hot air and supposed glamour and regimen in my life that it would seem impossible for him to want to be a part of it. And third, because I don't know what I believe in. I don't know what I want, or what's possible for me to want. I don't know if I believe in marriage and forever, and if that's the case, then how can I justify allowing another to love me or me to love?

But there are things I do know. I know he is gentle, at least for now. I also believe he is sincere, so I embrace him with my entire being and make him welcome in the quietest parts of myself, in places only I dwell in silent moments, alone.

⁓

5:45 A.M.

Driving in the dark through Texas. Venus hangs like an untouchable pearl that has urged on many travelers in pursuit of its elusive treasure. The sky looks like a bruise today. Blue and black, with a rim of blood-orange on the horizon.

He is quiet while he drives. He awoke at four A.M. to finish up the work I try to keep him from doing during the day, if I can help it. We're coming to a crossroads again. He's off to a rodeo; I'm expected at a show in Atlanta. But I would be content just to drive all day. Just hit the accelerator going past Dallas–Fort Worth and drive straight into the day as it awakens. Today I don't want to be a star. I want to be quiet, fold myself in like the wings of a sparrow, and watch the jagged outline of the hills come slowly into focus. I know that in the end, I will go where I must—but not without the scent of sagebrush and dry earth still in my hair.

But for now, my cowboy drives us the two hours to the airport. His silhouette contemplative, watching the road. "I love you," he says quietly. I love him. Who knows where the road leads hearts like ours? But this morning it is enough to know I am in love and watch the sun rise through the black trees, not knowing what lies beyond each turn.

CHAPTER 3

My dad told me that some of the most important things a person can know in the world are how to handle an animal, survive on the land, and trade sweat for fence posts.

Ty was running out of grass because it hasn't rained in Texas all sum-
mer. It's been a hot one. The land is scorched and brown and dry and
thirsty. Water holes have dried up and a lot of ranchers have had to
start using their hay for feed, which is an unexpected expense, one that
for some of them could mean the difference between breaking even and
being broke. Ty decided to ship the calves early to conserve grass. What
was left would feed the cows and bulls till winter. This meant rounding
up the cattle, sorting the calves from cows, then separating grown
calves from smaller late arrivals, which were unshippable. Then loading
the marked calves on trucks, and vaccinating, branding, earmarking,
and dehorning the smaller ones.

There were two cooks who arrived first, in the darkness, at 5:30 A.M.
The cowboys started straggling in shortly after, one by one or in pairs.
There were seven total, including a boy of fourteen named Bud and a
businessman friend of Ty's who could ride but who had never been on a
roundup. Then there was me—the eighth—the only girl. I had worked
with cattle as a kid, but I had never roped or done the "men's" work.

In Alaska, roundup took place in wide-open country where there
was lots of brush for the cattle to hide in. But in these tidy fields, the
roundup was easy. My horse took to bucking in the river bottom, chas-
ing some strays across the stream. But not hard bucking; I was able to
hang on till he straightened his head again and continued trotting as if
the whole thing had just been a bit of exercise. I joined the others, no
one the wiser. My horse hunched up again when we were all together
driving the cattle to a gate, but it wasn't much, just a bit of "pig snout-
ing," as they say in Australia.

Ty has a nice setup. Plenty of pens with interconnecting gates for
sorting and moving the cattle and a good loading chute. First we pushed
all 460 mother cows and calves into a large pen, then we began to sort
the cows out, leaving the calves in the pen. To sort, you ride in a full
pen and "roll" the cows off, by picking them out and away from the oth-
ers, moving them into a separate pen. Two of us picked them out and
one held the gate, discouraging the renegade calves from following their
mothers. Then a couple of cowboys cut the small calves from the big
ones and penned them in groups of similar size. It was only eight A.M.
at this point and the sun was already blistering. The trucks came and
loaded about a hundred head.

It was time to start doctoring. It takes some doing to work on a calf. First, a roper "heels" it by lassoing the hind feet and drags it to the five-man ground crew. Two cowboys hold the calf down. Another man dehorns the calf. Doing this ensures the calves will never wound themselves or each other with their sharp horns. Still another "earmarks" the calf. One man vaccinates while another brands and castrates. It's like an auto-racing pit crew. If everyone has one job, the whole overhaul can be done in two or so minutes.

I started the day as a roper, snaring calves with Chuck and Cody. Cody was the real roper; Chuck and I were learning. I am a little better at heading—roping the animal's neck—than "trapping" the back feet. Consequently, I caught one around the hips, one by one back leg, one by the neck, and finally, one by both back legs . . . you get the picture. When I got off to let a better roper at it, I vaccinated with the ground crew. The guys showed me how to jab a needle quickly under the calf's "armpit," squeeze, and pull out. It takes seconds.

Ty was earmarking, dehorning, and castrating. He would slit the sack with a sharp pocketknife, strip the testicles, and cut all in less than a minute. Those poor calves got the works that day. A couple calves got released before they were earmarked, so after we finished and ate lunch, Cody and Bud went to find them. Bud was back a few minutes later with bad news: they'd found a calf with a broken leg. We went over to find Cody holding the squirming creature down.

If it had been an ankle break it could have been splinted. But it wasn't. It was a clean break above the hock on its back leg. And it was broken straight through the bone. If not for muscle and hide, the bone would have fallen clean off.

"It's done for. Hell. How'd you manage this?" Ty asked. Cody reported in a quiet voice that he had roped a front leg. The calf reared, turned, then he heard a pop. Cody thought it was a rock until the calf fell, got up, and fell again, its leg bent under unnaturally.

"I'll go get my pistol," Ty said. He came back with a 30/30 instead and shot the calf in the head. Then Cody and Bud went to drag it off to where the buzzards could make quick work of it.

It was now noon and hotter than hell. While the cooks cleaned up the campsite, the boys loaded up their horses and shot the breeze. I unsaddled the gray horse I'd been riding, which had a lot of good cow sense. Some horses are born with a lot of cow in them. They instinctively work and herd cattle, almost like a collie. He was soaked in sweat and I was glad to take the heavy saddle off him.

We said thanks and good-bye to everyone, and went back to the house to shower and maybe nap before we drove to Clifton to watch the calves sell.

No cowgirl today - I don't wanna be.

I should be excited. I'm on my way to attend the premiere of my first film, Ride with the Devil. I get to dress up and have cocktails with a group of film industry people at the Toronto Film Festival. So why am I dreading the awkward conversation, the obligatory compliments, the covert—and not so covert—stares? The truth is, I'm not crazy about dressing up, the never-ending search for yet another dress, and the constant vigilance that goes into trying not to end up in some gossip column as a fashion "don't." It's strange getting used to the fishbowl.

I can't believe my life sometimes. Yesterday I was working cattle and today I'm off to my movie premiere.

Two Days Off

The cold light of the moon hid behind scattered clouds. But the stars were bright and the crickets loud as I stepped out beyond the reach of the taillights' red glow. Crisp mountain air filled my lungs, which for so long have been filled with smog and other people's cigarettes, bus fumes, and jet fuel. Tonight it was the honest smells of mountain air and fresh pine as two salty cowboys drove me through the Sierra mountains, the headlights of the old pickup truck parting the darkness like Moses parted the Red Sea.

We pulled over at the top of a pass and I hopped up on the flatbed to sing songs in the darkness. My fingers knew the cold strings blind. Melody rose out of my depths and poured out into the dark waters of midnight. No sharp edges could be seen to distract. My face a black shadow. And so I sang for the three of us and for all the dark trees that swayed like proud soldiers and for the mountains and the moon. My voice, my small single voice, added itself to the wind and to the sound of nothing, to the river and to the rock and the crickets and the creaking pines, and I didn't feel outside my life, larger and magnified by stage lights and microphones and magazines, exaggerated by headlines and TV specials, but in proportion, a small flame holding her candle in the darkness. No less, no more.

My grandmother was studying to become an opera singer, but instead she decided, were she to have children, they must be born in a new land: Alaska.

She was raised in Switzerland, but was living in Germany just before World War II, studying voice. Her boyfriend, Pegus, was part of a group of informed, progressive thinkers who called themselves "futurists." People who, they hoped, would pioneer the future. With war on the horizon, the young futurists began to look for new opportunities in new lands. They were disappointed to find that there was little real frontier left, but in America there was still one more untamed region— Alaska. Alaska was still a territory. It was wide open and challenging and free, the way they envisioned their lives would be away from the oppressive political climate in Germany. Rumor was that the territory was ripe for homesteading; that is, land would be given to those stalwart souls who were willing to clear, work, and populate it. It was a deal a group of young idealists couldn't refuse. They sent one young man ahead to scout out land where they might settle.

A year later the group received word that the scout had found the perfect place. But by this time they had become so absorbed in work and life at home that they no longer wanted to relocate. Only Ruth, my grandmother, remained enchanted by the emancipating prospects of Alaska. She loved Pegus yet she felt her destiny was in Alaska, where no threats of war would reach her and her future family. She left Pegus and her voice lessons and put herself on a ship to Alaska. When she arrived in Seward, she was met by the scout—my grandfather, Yule Kilcher—who presented her with a bouquet of flowers and a proposal of marriage. She accepted, and set about making and raising a family in the middle of the roughest wild country in the world.

My grandmother canned food, baled hay, cleared forests, and home-educated her children, but she never neglected her creativity. She began to sharpen her writing skills and became one of the first female journalists in Alaska. Her articles gained her national attention, and she was recognized for her work by two presidents—Franklin Roosevelt and Lyndon Johnson.

When I was sixteen I visited her in Louisville, Kentucky, where she was living with her new husband. She was lovely, with high cheekbones and green eyes that looked nearly translucent, her blond hair piled on her head. She showed me the photographs taken of her with the presidents. She read me two of her newest poems, and gave me books containing her older ones. Then she told me that she didn't fear death (she had recently been ill) because she felt that she had been reborn: she had seen all of her dreams come alive in her grandchildren. Our successes were validating for her, she said, because she had postponed some of her immediate desires to invest in the future of her family.

❧

Today I sang with Merle Haggard at the Country Music Awards. I feel lucky that this is my life! I have been able to meet, work, and tour with so many talented people. People whom I have admired and been inspired by for a long time. Merle has had something like fifty-six number one hits, fifty-four of which he wrote himself. That's amazing. We sang "That's the Way Love Goes" for the show. He was everything I hoped: talented, very nice, and still in love with music more than anything. More than the business of music. I learned a lot being around him—what to do and definitely what not to do.

I love seeing writers and players who have kept their integrity. Touring with Bob Dylan was that same way. Having him and Merle recite to me their favorite lyrics of mine was something I'll be telling my grandkids about. Dylan's favorite song was "Who Will Save Your Soul?" Merle liked "Pieces of You." Who would have thought?

It's an honor to be part of awards shows. I remember the first time I went to the Grammys. It seemed unreal. A "This is definitely not Alaska anymore, Toto" experience. I just couldn't believe I was not only in attendance but also a nominee. I went from living on five dollars a day to attending the industry's biggest event in a $14,000 dress that had been given to me by a designer for the occasion. Poltz had flown in to be there; my dad came wearing his town cowboy hat and leather vest, and I don't remember having seen my mom that dressed up before. She looked beautiful. The entire evening was great. I sat next to Lyle Lovett and Sting, for heaven's sake!

I still feel that sense of awe and gratitude to think I am so privileged, surrounded by so many people I respect.

❧

When I was twenty and first began touring, I felt like a stranger in a strange land. Overnight, I went from being a surf rat to doing forty cities in thirty days. We'd drive all night, sleep two hours, show up at some high school, do a show for kids who were only glad to see us because it got them out of class, do press, go to the local radio station and beg them to play my record, go to a local record store and play for the eleven people who were there buying someone else's records, do a show that night as an opening act, hand out flyers announcing the coffeehouse where I'd be appearing at midnight, do the coffeehouse gig, then drive all night again.

I was challenged and excited to have a chance to sing every day. But it wasn't glamorous. All I saw of the world was sleazy club owners, handfuls of goths who talked through my material, and radio people who couldn't wait to break the news to me that I didn't stand a chance—didn't I realize I was competing with Nirvana and Soundgarden at their height? I started saving every dime I made, as if it was the last money that'd ever come my way. But I also started getting off on the adversity. I started wondering just how far a dark horse could go.

❧

On the homestead we ate what we raised. Potatoes. Lots of potatoes. Endless fields of them we planted and weeded by hand, then stored beneath our house just before the first freeze. Every manner of vegetable. Rose hips and raspberries for jam. Fresh milk and cream we turned into butter, cottage cheese, and yogurt. Occasionally we'd make whipped cream to put on fruit or pancakes. Once Yule successfully grew a very small crop of wheat, which supplied us for many years to come. I'd blow the husks off of a handful of golden berries, then grind them into flour using an old-fashioned grinder we had. We'd cook pancakes and bake bread from scratch, made from fresh eggs, fresh milk, and fresh flour.

Yule had a fifty-year-old sourdough starter. It was given to him by a famous Alaskan pioneer. With it he made thick, dense sourdough bread that was nearly black from the many "extras" he'd add. Nettles. Leftover soup. Garden weeds. Who knows what all. Suffice it to say I preferred my dad's bread over Yule's. Food shouldn't be a guessing game.

We gathered salmon from nets and, during the warm summer months, harvested coal for heat off the beach. And in the fall, we always butchered a few cattle. Some of the meat we sold but the rest we saved for winter.

I know that slaughtering time seems incomprehensible to people who have seen meat only laid out in little foam trays, encased in shiny plastic. But on a farm, autumn is harvest time—and butchering season is another beat in the rhythm of the year. We'd gut and bleed the animal while it was hanging upside down. My grandpa would collect all the blood in a large white bucket he set under the animal's nose. He'd use that to make an old-world delicacy called blood sausage.

We were always careful to use every part of the animal. (That's why, when it was castrating time, everyone knew to avoid dinner invitations!) After the animal was skinned, we'd cut it into parts, wrap each cut in freezer paper, and label it. T-bone. Prime rib. Tongue. Heart and tongue were the first to be eaten because they were best fresh. Heart was okay. It tasted like liver. Given enough ketchup, it was tolerable, but tongue . . . well, that took some getting used to. It tasted fine, but the idea of eating an animal's tongue could be a bit overwhelming. My brothers and I found a solution, though. We would chop some up, mix it with mayonnaise, and make it into a tuna salad–type thing that we packed in our lunches. Then, at school, we'd convince kids they were tuna sandwiches and swap them for their pizza squares.

When we were little, our job was to cart the stomachs to the corner field in a wheelbarrow. There we popped them with a long skinny knife. The smell was obnoxious. But on a ranch, bad smells don't really faze you. It's just how it is. At night the wolves would come and carry the guts away. From the window, with the lights off, you could see their iridescent eyes floating in the darkness.

The first time we were around at slaughtering time, my brother Shane was old enough to help, Atz could watch, but Dad told me I was not allowed to watch at all. The fact that I might not want to watch didn't occur to me. I felt like somehow my rights were being threatened. Atz was younger, so why would he get to watch? Was I being singled out because I was the only girl on the farm? No chance!

I snuck up into the hayloft and snuggled into a spot where I could see clearly every detail of the events below. My father held a rifle and stood next to my uncle to my left. The cow was below me and to my right. She was staring at my dad and uncle with round, soft eyes. Then, *bam!* The cow was still standing. My dad fired again. And again. Now the cow listed awkwardly to one side, then finally dropped. I don't think there was a dry eye in the barnyard and I wished I hadn't been watching. I got off the hay pile and went into the yard.

The men had dragged the cow with the tractor to the hitching tree, leaving a trail of blood behind that the dogs followed, licking. It all seemed so terrible. Then they slit the cow's belly. A pile of translucent guts spilled out. I noticed my dad staring quietly into the cavity. He was visibly upset. My uncle muttered, "Damn." Shane was quiet. Then my little brother, Atz, started kicking my father's shins with all the fury a skinny six-year-old could muster, yelling, "You cow murderer! You cow murderer!"

I came closer. Inside the carcass was curled a tiny embryonic calf. "That's why she wouldn't go down," my father whispered to my uncle Otto, fighting to hold back tears. He shook his head. We were always very careful about which animals we bred. We would never endanger an animal that could be pregnant. Some bull must have broken through the fence from an adjoining field. It happens.

My dad scooped out the tiny embryo and we put it in a jar to take to school for science class. The teacher was excited to have a new visual aid. And it didn't seem the least bit strange to the other kids. Around those parts, death was just as vivid and present as life.

❧

We had a goat once. It was impossible to take care of.
It ate its own chain. We had to tether it in the

middle of the yard so it wouldn't eat the siding off of our house. It would butt and kick you if you wandered too close. I was almost glad when it came time to slaughter it. I didn't care for the meat, though. It was tough and greasy with bits of hair stuck in it.

During an early tour supporting *Pieces of You*, I stumbled up to my room after traveling all night to Boston by bus. I was so sleepy I hardly noticed the ambulance parked quietly outside the hotel door.

I got off the elevator on the third floor and hoisted my heavy bag over my shoulder. How did I always manage to get the room that was located as far from the elevator as was scientifically possible? My black duffel bag thumped against my heels and leg and I limped down endless puke-green corridors. But when I rounded yet another corner, following the arrow that promised to deliver me to ROOMS 350–374, I happened upon a scene that brought me to a slow crawl.

There, about halfway down the hall, were two men in burgundy polyester hotel attire huddled with two others dressed in paramedic white, and together they were all trying to gain entry into room 364, which appeared to be chained shut from the inside. The men hardly noticed me as I thumped past with my awkward baggage. Through the crack in the door I could see green and orange shaggy carpet and one leg of a dark brown Formica coffee table.

"Mr. Fernman . . . Mr. Fernman . . . are you in there?" they called into the space between the door and jamb.

A walkie-talkie in someone's pocket crackled; a pair of wire cutters were on their way up. I slogged to my room and inserted the key into the lock. I wondered who Mr. Fernman was. I wondered whether he had slipped in the shower and couldn't get up or if he jumped out the fire escape without paying his bill or if he pulled that official tag that said DO NOT REMOVE off of his mattress.

That night, on my way to the gig, I asked Todd, the young man who was on duty at the desk, what he would rather be: a working tractor or a really cool hot rod that didn't run anymore. He told me he would rather be the car. I asked him why. He told me he would prefer to be the car because a broken-down hot rod did less work than a functioning tractor. I looked him over and decided it made sense.

"Hey," I said, heading for the door, "what went on here this morning—with the paramedics and all that?"

Todd looked around, signaled me to come closer, and whispered, either somewhat spooked or out of respect, "I'm not supposed to talk about it, but some guy hung himself upstairs."

I pushed the door open and headed into the street. Next time I'm in Boston, I've got to remember: request any room but 364.

⤝

DFW to the Ranch

The Texas countryside is parched. I have two days off between shows. I left my band behind in Columbus, Ohio. I'll catch up with them in Atlanta. Here the grass is gold for miles, with splashes of brittle green shrub and oak brush. It is 9:40 A.M. and it is already 103 degrees, which means it's just gonna keep getting hotter. My car flies by abandoned barns and run-down girly clubs and driving ranges on a narrow country road. Spotted ponies stand listless in burned fields. There are old stone houses that look like broken-down relics with brand-new Ford Tauruses parked out front.

Big John's Wood Products looks like the heart of one small settlement that gathers itself along the 138 like so many indistinguishable look-alike towns. The Gulch Family Fun Park. Bible Baptist Church. Niesters Deli and Restaurant. A little blue barbershop whose sign reads simply BARBER SHOP in big red letters. Here Hennington's Famous BBQ Palace is a small shack and Tru-Life Taxidermy shares its small block of parking spaces with Kroger's Groceries. And look—an ear, nose, and throat doctor has set up practice in an abandoned Denny's. Instead of a yellow Denny's sign on top of the A-frame, there's a plain white one that reads DOCTOR, ENT in somber black script. I'll take mine to go.

Now the flash of town recedes, almost as suddenly as it sprang into view. The roadside scenery is rural again until we get to Tolar. Tolar is a ghost town, left over from the oil-boom days, I suppose. All empty storefronts, except for the flea market and the Methodist church, the only two buildings that still haven't thrown off their last coat of paint. A whole town just picked up and abandoned its dreams. Or ran from them. Then, like that, we're past it. The countryside overtakes the road again in a never-ending rhythm of concrete intermittently winning and losing its battle with mud, sun, and weeds.

Dry riverbed with bits of tire scattered in the sun-bleached sand. A farmer in overalls and no shirt and a large straw hat, flapping his arms, coaxing a docile black milk cow back to its pen. Skinny horses that graze around rusted refrigerators, car parts, and gutted-out washing machines.

⊸

"Why won't you take a sponge bath, Jewel?" my father would say to me, exasperated, completely at a loss. To him it was nothing. Need a sponge bath, take a sponge bath.

Why don't I *like* to take a sponge bath? Could it be because I'm a teenager who lives with a houseful of men and boys? Could it be because our door doesn't even have a doorknob, much less a lock? Or maybe it's the idea of stripping naked and standing in a tiny bucket of soapy water in the middle of the kitchen/living room while everyone else waits impatiently upstairs or outside for me to finish my underarms and towel off? Did I really need to explain any of this?

"Why not, Jewel? Just tell me why . . ."

I'd stare at him stubbornly, too proud or embarrassed to explain.

On the homestead, sponge baths and the once-a-week, need-it-or-not Sunday-night sauna were pretty much it for personal hygiene options, except in the summer. When the weather got warm, Yule would prop three skinny wooden poles together like a tepee skeleton and run a garden hose to it from the stream near the garden. He'd thread the hose straight up the poles then attach a watering can spout to one end. The spout kind of dripped and sprinkled and gurgled springwater where the beneficiary of Yule's ingenuity was to stand. The only problem was that the water was ice-cold, so you practically had hypothermia by the time your hair conditioner was in. And since the shower was right in the middle of the pasture near Yule's house, there wasn't much privacy, either. Not that it bothered Yule. "Privacy? Why so modest?" To him, we were all animal flesh, he said, just like the horses and cows. Maybe so. But I had seen how men looked at women in town, and it wasn't the way they looked at cows. Well, maybe a good horse . . .

All the neighbors within twenty miles would come for their weekly sauna, like sausages to a smokehouse. It wasn't like communal perspiration was considered a pastime in Alaska; it was just a matter of necessity. Hardly anyone had plumbing out that far, and it was simply energy-efficient to start one wood-fired sauna big enough for a bunch of people once a week.

Yule's sauna was the best. It was a tiny wood-slat cabin that sat next to a small, four-foot-deep, hand-dug pond covered in visqueen. When you got too hot you could jump in the ice-cold, algae-lined pond. So, once a week, I was treated to the sight of cousins, uncles, neighbors, all stripped and sweaty like pigs. But I didn't join them. I'd wait until everyone else was through, even though the sauna wouldn't be very hot anymore. Living with all those men, privacy was hard to find. It was an issue I would have loved to have been able to complain about to my friends . . . if only we had had a private phone line.

My family shared our telephone line with about six neighbors. Consequently, when you picked up the handset to make a call, you might not get a dial tone. Instead you might get Carol talking with some person about gardening or Bob fighting with his wife or Annette sneaking a call to a boyfriend. Sometimes when you were on the phone you'd hear someone pick up then hang up with a clatter. That was a subtle hint that someone on the party line needed to use the phone—and that it seemed to them that their call was more important than yours. Of course, there were always those people who picked up quietly, with a barely discernible click. If you were paying attention, you could tell that someone was eavesdropping. If you weren't paying attention, they'd get an earful.

Not that there are many secrets in a small town.

People can get just as desperate and sad and burned-out in America's small towns as they do in cities. You just don't hear about it on the news. It's as if their stories just join the swirl of local gossip, circulate through town, and, ultimately, get nowhere.

In the summers following my parents' divorce, I began to do odd jobs for Emmy, a close family friend. She was an energetic ranch woman and like a second mother to me. I had my own bedroom at her house and I helped her with the horses, cooking, and cleaning—and anything else she'd let me do.

I'd known her son, Decker, since I was a small child. Since I'd stayed with them for so many summers, we'd grown quite close.

Decker was diagnosed with schizophrenia when he was eighteen or nineteen. It happened all of a sudden. At first we were hopeful for a cure. He was on a lot of medication, in and out of institutions. Eventually he moved out on his own and built a plywood cabin right next to where I was living by myself at age sixteen. He built it with his "crazy checks," which is how he referred to the monthly government subsidy he was receiving in exchange for being too unstable to hold a job.

We were pretty pleased when Decker got his own place. It was good to see him doing well and on his own. As a child I idolized him. He was smart, handsome, funny, and cool when I was still a scrawny kid. Gradually, I began to notice him change.

No one told me outright that Decker was schizophrenic. I think I was considered too young to digest that sort of news. But, slowly, Decker had become a universe unto himself. No one knew what was wrong with him at first. Once, when we were younger, he chased me around the house, bent over like a Neanderthal, his hair all messy and his blue eyes wide, mumbling, "I'm a medicine man . . . I'm a medicine man!" At first I thought it was funny, but then it became a little spooky. I knew that he wasn't kidding. Another time he was driving the car carrying his mom and me. He started out driving carefully enough but then he swerved into the oncoming lane of traffic, staring at the panic-stricken driver of each car as it made its way past us. At first Emmy laughed it off. ("Oh, Decker, come on now!") But when we all started feeling as terrified as the oncoming drivers looked, she made a grab for the wheel and managed to steer the car back into its own lane. Clearly, Decker's techniques did not conform to the Alaska state driving code. Still, it was a couple of years before his license was revoked.

Some days Decker was lucid and "within the grid." Other days he just wasn't. Unfortunately, you could never be sure with him just what kind of a day it would be. One time he went to an Ozzy Osborne concert, alone, in Anchorage. He caught a flight back to Homer and began to wig on the plane. He asked a stewardess for some Vaseline. When she found some for him, he grabbed it greedily, took off the lid, and smeared it all over his face. The flight crew was frightened. They called ahead to the Homer police. But when the police heard who was greasing himself up in economy, they said—oh . . . it's Decker! Don't worry, he's eccentric but totally harmless.

After he moved out to his cabin, he became kind of isolated. My little brother, Atz, and I would visit him. It was fun and definitely never boring. Once I picked Decker up hitchhiking on my way home. I don't think he recognized me. He just sat fidgeting in the passenger's seat, rocking and looking straight ahead. Finally I said, "Hey Decker, how's life?" He looked at me sideways, then ahead, and replied, "Ain't no bowl of fuckin' Froot Loops." Too right. We pulled up in front of his place to find my brother waiting at his door. Then the three of us stepped into his cabin.

Exploring Decker's cabin was like exploring another planet. The Sheetrock walls were unfinished. The floor was rough plywood, and dotted with ten or twelve neatly arranged mountains of dust. Piles so tidy I knew it must have taken Decker some time to sweep them just so. Monoliths in dust.

The countertop was a plywood panel balanced between two saw-horses. Strewn across the "counter" were an electric hot plate, an assortment of half-eaten food, books, a snarl of clothes, and a few cans of corned beef hash. Across the room, the same type of counter had been duplicated to serve as a table. It, too, was a smorgasbord of rubble, except for one corner where Decker kept his meds.

Over our heads, a ceiling fan/light combo ticked and wobbled, ticked and wobbled. Decker began to pace nervously.

"Gotta pee. Gotta pee. Can't pee. Gotta pee," Decker told me. He wore his pants inside out. The pockets flapped like soggy gun holsters. "Gotta pee."

Atz and I suggested he step outside, to the outhouse. He looked at us like we were crazy.

"Can't!" he blurted. "Blackfoot are out there. I can't!"

I groped for a frame of reference. Then I remembered a book I'd seen on his counter . . . a novel about Indians. By now he was getting frantic.

"Blackfoot outside. I'm Cherokee! They'll kill me."

Atz and I looked at each other. In Decker's mind the scenario was very real. He believed his life was in danger. He was reacting as anyone would who was experiencing this kind of a trauma. Now he was absolutely beside himself.

"Gotta pee!" he chanted, pacing. Then, suddenly, he stopped, mid-stride. "I know!" he said. "Pee pile! Pee in the pee pile!"

Then he turned his back to us and proceeded to relieve himself on one of the dust piles. A perfectly fantastic solution for a perfectly fantastic problem.

By this time, I was looking to Atz for an exit vibe. But now Decker was opening the refrigerator, his torso naked and unearthly in the greenish glow of the refrigerator light. He briefly surveyed the contents of the fridge; his slack, unused body bent like a bow. Then, from the chaos of open cans and aging leftovers, he produced a quart of melted strawberry ice cream. Ceremoniously, he took off the lid and dipped two fingers into the cold soup. Then, with reverence, he began to apply his "war paint"—stripes along his cheeks, stripes on each arm, then a healthy smear across the torso. Pleased and very quiet, he turned to Atz and me. He stared. We stared. Then he said, "Okay, I'm invisible now. I can go outside."

That was our cue. Atz and I told Decker that it was good to have seen him and we said we'd stop by again soon. Then we got into my little car. We would come back. I loved to read his writing. Decker is a very good writer and a very sweet and gentle person.

I don't write these things about Decker to make fun of him or to make him sound strange. Decker is the sweetest and, oddly, one of the most honest people I know. He has always been super-aware that he makes people uncomfortable. He knows that he has a disease that affects his brain and that he can't control it. He's aware that he may never have a girlfriend like other people even though he'd like one.

This often causes him to avoid people because he's aware that they stare and whisper. It is sad to me that there isn't more help or understanding about schizophrenia. Those who are affected by it are simply given meds and left on their own. I wish there were some way we could heal him and bring him comfort the way he continues to bring comfort to the people near him.

A friend called to wish him a Merry Christmas.

"Merry Christmas," he said.

"Well, actually, I don't feel very merry," Decker's friend replied. (Her father had died recently and this would be her first Christmas without him.)

Decker was quiet a moment. Then he said, "That's okay. Sometimes even just a little bit merry is enough. You don't always have to feel the whole deal."

❧

The young gangsters in Tokyo, impeccable and dapper, but missing a few fingers.

The three Frenchmen in first class who consider taunting the stewardess a form of "in-flight entertainment."

The homeless lady, scamming the ladies'-room line in Grand Central, charging people twenty-five cents to use the public rest room.

One of my greatest joys in life has been sitting quietly, pen in hand, observing the people with whom I share the world. But now when I look at them, they're already looking at me.

⊗

Day Off Between Columbus and Cleveland

Spent the day in another world. It was just a day. Noon to noon. But it was enough to make me forget everything. Ty and I swam in a big lake that was warm as bathwater. Then he put a .22 and .38 in old leather holsters around my hips and we drove to a dry riverbed to shoot little orange targets. It was my first time shooting and I fared pretty well.

We rode horses all across his 1,800 acres. It was over a hundred degrees and so hot and oppressive in places it sucked the breath from your lungs. But the cattle were fat and shiny and the yearlings were strong and filled out and it was all so much to see. When we were finally worn out, we straggled into the shop where Ty keeps his mechanical bull. He put his bronc saddle on it and I climbed on. He showed me how to sit and move and keep contact and when to stroke back. He manipulated the machine manually while I got my bearings. He'd pull the nose down and I'd lean back, feet pointed out, hard up. Then he'd point the nose to the sky. I'd lean forward, pivot my legs at the knees then set my feet forward to be ready before it broke over again.

By this time I was covered in sweat and starving. We drove to town, where, in a little house, there is a one-room café just big enough for eight plywood tables. There is only one meal on the menu each day, and if you like it, you stay; if you don't, you leave. Cheese enchiladas. Chunky mashed potatoes with hot dogs sliced into them. Canned peas cooked beyond recognition in a Crock-Pot with butter and salt. And a slice of spice cake. We stayed.

⊗

Camping in the Sierras

Rode with some cowboys high in the Sierras. Camped next to a stream. Pat told stories about good rides and wild cattle and the sorrow of so much open space being swallowed up and I drifted off to sleep while the music of the river and the half-moon worked their magic on the pines.

I am one of the last of America's children to be raised with a first-hand feel for the pioneer spirit. Alaska was the last territory settled, just fifty years ago. My father was raised a pioneer's son and I, his daughter, was raised on that same land.

I miss working with my hands. I think back to those steamy days, canning rose hips on the coal stove. Boiling the preserves in huge vats of hot water—preparing for the cold, long days of winter.

Some nights, usually in a hotel far from home, I imagine myself behind the wheel of the tractor. Do I remember what it feels like to start it, to hear it clatter to life? Do I remember how to crank the old Ford by hand and shift the gears?

❧

Spain
Drop to my knees
such beauty
reminds me
each day
we waken
anew

❧

My best friend,
Jacque, used to
say, "Sleep beneath
the stars and you
will wake with more
answers than you
had questions to."

photos i've taken

Roping arena, Texas

Grain barn

90-year-old cedar barn

Ty getting ready to rope

Horse in Texas

Horses in Las Vegas

The waiting room

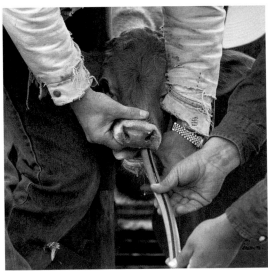

Getting doctored

This year's crop

A few months before branding

Steer in the chute

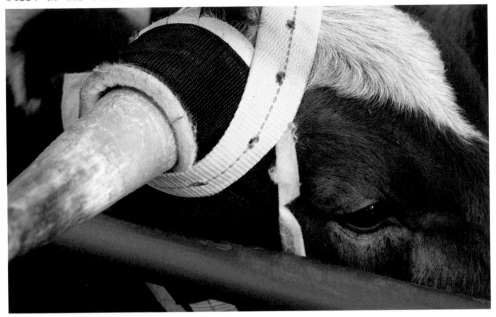

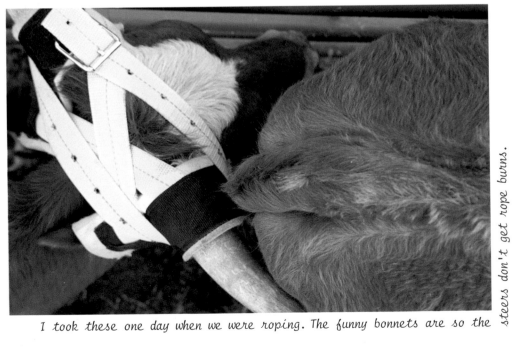

I took these one day when we were roping. The funny bonnets are so the steers don't get rope burns.

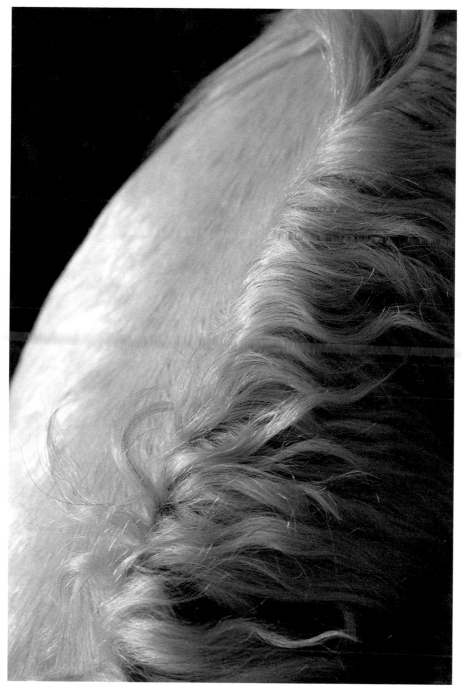

Grey, Ty's horse

Hawaii

Hawaii

The Big Island

Scotland

Airport, St. Paul, Minnesota

Las Vegas

Chinatown, San Francisco

New York

Airport, Phoenix, Arizona

Video arcade, Las Vegas

CHAPTER *4*

*T*here are all sorts of famous
stories that surround a person,
like mysterious robes, making the
human invisible and the image
super-real.

As a teenager, I prided myself on my ability to seem blasé about every-thing, impossible to shock or surprise. Somehow I got it in my head that appearing too interested or engaged in what was going on around me made me seem unsophisticated. So when I announced—at age six-teen—that I would travel alone, by thumb, bus, and train, to see my mom in Mexico, where she was vacationing, and that I would fund this adventure by working as a street singer, I played it cool. Mexico? No big deal. Just another trip to the grocery store.

Immediately I started planning and gathering everything I knew I'd need, like a comfortable hiker's pack and a decent sleeping bag. I set aside money to pay for these things from my ongoing gig at a local club in Interlochen, Michigan, where I sang on weekends while I was going to school. Since I still lacked sufficient funds to pay for a trip to and through Mexico, busking—performing in parks or on street corners for donations—seemed a logical solution. But that introduced another quandary: I needed accompaniment. I would have to learn to play gui-tar. How hard could it be?

As it turned out, it was too difficult for me to memorize other musicians' patterns and chords. It seemed much easier just to make up my own. So I set about writing myself a repertoire. *Money. Soul. Billy. Raven.*

As spring break neared, I had all the details worked out. I would Greyhound it from Interlochen to Detroit, then take a train three days cross-country to San Diego to meet my friend from Alaska, Mary, who was a sea captain. We would cross into Tijuana, fly to Topolobampo, grab a train to Chihuahua, then meet my mom where she was hiking in Copper Canyon. After our visit, Mary and I would ferry to La Paz and, after a week of R&R, hitchhike back to Tijuana, where I would board a train back to Michigan then take a bus back to school. No problem.

I was blinded by my overconfidence. I was grown up and indepen-dent. I reveled in pretending that I wasn't in school at all. As far as my fellow passengers knew, I was a self-sufficient woman. When they in-quired as to my travels, I tossed off the details of my complicated itinerary with nonchalance. When they acted impressed, I responded with a classic Barney Fife shrug. "Yeah, well . . ."

I was somewhere around Detroit when the man in the seat in front of me—a gruff and gritty guy with a bandanna over his young, weary face—turned to me out of the blue. "A lot of girls tell me they orgasm when they ride on a Harley," he declared.

I looked at him. Clearly, I was not so worldly-wise, after all. There were still some things I did not know. This orgasm thing, apparently, was one of them. "Oh," I responded flatly, staring into my book. I resented being baited.

Long pause.

"I have a Harley," he said plainly. His invitation lacked promise and enthusiasm.

I stared at him expressionless, until, at last, the man looked away. I turned from him without any sign of concern, though really my head was spinning. What a sick thing to say! How dare he make me feel like I was only sixteen! I doubled my resolve not to appear naive. It was impossible.

I made it to the train in Detroit and was pleased to know we'd be reaching Chicago just in time for me to busk there on St. Patty's Day. The wearing o' the green skirt turned out to be quite lucrative. I even got interviewed by a local news crew. They gave me some airtime as a performer, then asked me the ins and outs of busking parades. All in all, it was a very successful first day. I caught the train as it moved on toward San Diego, my guitar case burdened with at least fifty dollars' worth of quarters.

On that leg of the trip, I met a guy named Jeff who played guitar. Since I knew only three chords, and poorly, too, I had him show me some new ones . . . new strums, etc. Jeff told me he was ticketed for the whole three-day ride. He thought it would be interesting if I dropped acid with him and some friends.

I had heard lots of people talk about how much fun acid was and I thought, *What the heck.* I'd never done anything like it. I had never been stoned or drunk in my life, but I decided that the train was a safe place to try what I had been assured would be "a small dose." Jeff explained what would happen to me—how I could expect to feel—then gave me a small piece of paper that I was to place in my mouth.

At first I felt nothing, then I began to giggle. I had to pee, so I got up. That's when I realized I was in trouble. I got no further than the bathroom mirror. I was stuck in my own reflection. When Jeff noticed I was missing, he guessed where I might be. Since the door was unlocked, he let himself in and pried me from my self-hypnosis. Then he began kissing me. It was alarming and I began hating the high. I hated that I didn't want him to kiss me and that the drug made me foggy. I pulled away from him and found the mushroom/flashlight/gnome that was the doorknob. I left him in the bathroom with the mirror while I went upstairs to the bubble car to watch the scenery fly by. Eventually Jeff joined me and we watched his hand flutter on the neck of his guitar like a spider on a horizontal web.

I was struggling for control of my brain. I hated how stupidly I was behaving. Then an Indian chief boarded in Arizona and began to lecture on the significance of the land to his people. I had been taught to be respectful of elders and their wisdom. I felt awful, but the high made it impossible to stop laughing. I could see we were making the chief uncomfortable and that he was nervous and embarrassed, but I could not stop being loud. I had given the drug control over me. It was forcing emotion from me I didn't really feel. I couldn't wait to be normal again. I couldn't believe people enjoyed this.

Coming down was awful. My teeth ached. My muscles felt like the inside of a machine shop before they hosed it down—full of metal and oil that had lost its viscosity. I wrote painful twisted poems and became depressed. In the end, the high wasn't worth it. I had friends in school who were painters but couldn't paint unless they were high. It was as if they had no creativity sober. When I was high, I didn't feel the drug took me anywhere my creativity hadn't already taken me. I had experienced that my own mind and imagination could take me a lot higher. I haven't been interested in drugs since.

The rest of the trip went completely according to plan, hitchhiking and all. I sang in restaurants for supper and gave foot rubs to blue-hairs for cash. On the long ride back to Michigan, I thought about Harleys and acid and all the homework I had to catch up on. Since my train pulled into Detroit late and the next bus didn't leave until the morning, I spent the last night of my vacation in the Detroit Greyhound station. But it wasn't the shady characters that drove me nuts that night: it was the Muzak that blared continuously in the empty depot. I wondered whether there was anywhere in the building I could escape it. As I shut my eyes and listened to an incredibly soulless version of a Tracy Chapman tune, I wondered if one day there'd be another girl sitting in a chair in this bus station listening to one of *my* songs.

I slept uneasily, slumped in a chair, my backpack and trusty guitar at my side. For the first time I was writing my own songs, and I loved it. I loved the unpredictability and adventure of it all, and I was excited to see where else my life and my music might take me.

~

Tour Bus—Somewhere, Ohio

The road hisses by. I will never again be so young as I am now. I look in the mirror on the bus as I write. Still fresh-faced and not hardened. But each lamppost that passes outside, each mile, each minivan-minivan-minivan that blasts by on the highway takes with it seconds of my attention, minutes of my mindfulness, and hours of my life. Each truck stop and show and airport and heartache and victory shaves away at what is left of my feeling of newness, so that now I am wondering: *Am I spending my time wisely?* I only possess each second, each moment once, and if I am not conscious of each moment then I do not possess it at all. Am I wasting myself on something false? On pettiness, jealousy, fear, or empty thought? On pop stardom? Am I proud of how I've lived so far? When I take the final inventory of my life, will this moment be vivid and significant or just another forgettable detail in a long dull dream?

I peek through a corner of the window onto the streets flying by. How I long to be more conscious, more aware, more alive, not wasting myself on things that take me farther from myself like hatred, fear, worry, and gossip, but constantly reinvesting my energy in the things that make me feel vital . . . like being still . . . like writing what I know is real rather than what I know will make a hit . . . like kissing a man in the humid rain showers of Texas . . . and learning to love all people as I love God and all things.

~

When I was fourteen or fifteen, my dad and I went to play with a guitarist friend, Dan, at a biker bar called Tradewinds in Anchorage. For me, the place was quite an eyeful. Hogs of every make and model were lined up along a horsehitch, western style, beneath a neon sign that blinked out a pink palm tree and the name of the joint.

There were two men outside by the door helping a friend throw up. He was foaming at the mouth and convulsing, but I knew not to stare. I just peeked out of the corner of my eye as we hurried by.

Inside, the scene was surprisingly mellow. There were big men in black leather playing pool or drinking quietly by the bar. The bikers liked our music and were more enthusiastic than other crowds I'd played. They actually listened. The gig was a good time until, about forty minutes into the set, some very bright lights began flashing outside. I was about to ask what they were when my dad leaned over and whispered in my ear, "Why don't you go to the bathroom and wait there for a while. Just don't come out till I send for you." So off I went.

I hadn't waited long when a couple of ladies came in to keep me company. "Bobby said to make sure you were fine," one of them explained. I had no idea who Bobby was but told them thanks. Then we began to pass the time, chatting and looking at ourselves in the mirror. The ladies looked tired and smart. They fussed with their hair and applied more black liner around their eyes.

My dad had always been very insistent that, as performers, we be professional, well dressed, and presentable. But I was a fourteen-year-old homesteader. And homesteaders with very limited resources weren't known to have a cutting-edge sense of style. I was dressed in a white, long-sleeved shirt primly buttoned to the top. I think it even had beige kitty paw prints on it. My hair was plain, long, and straight. I felt painfully awkward and shy—especially around ladies who had fully developed their "look." But the lady Bobby sent was kind and protective. When she saw me fussing awkwardly with my buttons, she fixed my collar and reassured me. "This is a very nice shirt." She sounded like she wasn't used to giving compliments. Somehow the words made her seem fragile. "It looks nice on you."

By now the other lady had put the lid down and perched on the toilet in one of the only stalls. She sat there, door open, fussing with her nails. I hopped up on the counter. Then the lady on the toilet said in a thick, dull voice, "You know, honey, you should sing at my wedding. Yeah. Mike and I, we're finally getting hitched." Then she half grunted and added, "The bastard." She was quiet a bit. The fluorescent bulb made us all look pale, seasick.

"So you will, right?" she continued. "It'll be next May. The twelfth."

"I'll have to ask my dad," I said politely. Hoping my dad wouldn't mind. Wondering if she was serious.

I liked the two ladies. They made me feel safe. They told me about themselves, about their lives on the road. They told me a lot of things, things maybe a fourteen-year-old didn't need to know. But I was fascinated. Finally I asked what was going on outside. They said the heat had come and an ambulance had been called because a man was "f— I mean messed up on angel dust." I had no idea what angel dust might be, though it had a nice name.

About thirty minutes had passed before I heard my dad calling in after me. The pub patrons seemed a little stirred up, but everything was back to normal. The barkeep looked somber, unflappable, like he hadn't stopped wiping the bar even for a second, despite the hubbub. Several of the bikers came up to the stage to welcome me back. They bought me Shirley Temples. Then we finished the last three hours of the gig.

The bikers at the Tradewinds were very friendly and familial. I always felt safe around them. Protected. I know they were being careful not to curse around me and I appreciated their gentleness. They reminded me that we were all okay, just the way we were.

❧

Between the ages of eight and sixteen I lived for various lengths of time in many different houses—urban and rural—trailers, and cabins. From sixteen to nineteen I lived in several other houses, dorms, apartments—and, of course, one now-famous car.

It gets confusing, and at times I can't even remember which house came when. All I know for sure is that I led a pretty stable life until my parents divorced. Basically, before the divorce, we lived in Anchorage. After the divorce, we lived with my father on the family homestead in the small town of Homer. Then, when I was in the eighth grade, I went to live with my mother in Anchorage again. After so many years in the country, the city was a different world.

People think that being poor is being poor, and that its effects are pretty much the same wherever it occurs. Personally, I'd take being poor in the country any day over being poor in the city. In a small town, the economy affects most everyone the same way—which is to say that the financial playing field is usually pretty even. If everyone is doing what they can to get by, the poor aren't set apart, marginalized, or humiliated. Plus it is possible for a poor person to feel land-rich in a rural community. There is a certain stability that comes from the understanding that the land will always take care of you, as long as you are healthy enough to work it. The move from open country to the crowded, isolating city made me feel like the earth had literally been pulled out from under me.

There were no locks on our doors on the homestead and the diverse groups of travelers who straggled across the threshold were immediately accepted as extended—if temporary—family. But in Anchorage, I couldn't even assume the kids I knew had parents who lived with them. Small gangs replaced families. And the kids I knew relied on their gangs—to look out for them, make sure they ate, and watch their backs—and it didn't really matter that they were putting their safety in the hands of kids who didn't even have all their adult teeth yet. No matter how irresponsible those kids might be, they were more reliable than the adults in their lives.

Cara, my best friend, was half African-American, half Aleut. She told me that when she was a small child her dad had her play a game he called "sticks." To play it, all she had to do was pick the stems from marijuana buds in a giant bag of pot. Cara's mother was a good woman who was working her way through a string of bad boyfriends. Some of them were violent. During the time I knew her, one of her boyfriends raped a runaway girl to whom Cara and her mom were renting a room for extra cash. Ken—the boyfriend—was gone that day and all of his meager belongings got packed into a single, plastic garbage bag and thrown out in the street.

Amir was half African-American and half white. But he hated all whites except for me and his mother. His dad was a boxer and beat the crap out of him and his younger brother and sister. Sometimes it was so bad they had to skip school. Kids who got beaten regularly knew to avoid school; teachers were mandated by the state to report any cases of suspected child abuse. Not even the kids wanted the state involved in their business.

Vinnie hung around with us, too, until he got mixed up in gangs after school. Believe it or not, the Bloods and Crips had become very prevalent in Anchorage at that time. Vinnie had a leg amputated as a result of a gang-related fight.

As for me, I was a grubby homestead girl who sang in pubs, got by in school, swore a lot, and smelled like a farm. At least that's what the popular kids said.

We all had dreams of getting out, making it big. My friends all said I was going to be the next Whitney Houston.

≈

Taiwan

In Taipei, I was ushered to a hotel room that was nearly a mansion in itself: it was furnished with graceful, hand-painted Asian furniture and stocked with a never-ending supply of chocolates and flowers.

The hotel management must have thought I was a princess or something, which was unusual considering that at the time I was nothing beyond the American market. Every time I walked into the lobby, the staff and management would scurry to their feet, form two straight lines, and stand at attention as I walked between them. They even supplied me with a . . . a what? A handmaiden? A female butler, basically, who stood outside my door anytime I was in—and all night while I slept. As far as I know, this poor woman rested only when I went out to shop or do a show. I tried to refuse her service but the hotel wouldn't hear of it. Whenever I peeked out my door, there she was, standing at attention.

Taipei, I discovered, was fame's waiting room. The clubs were filled with almost-pretty-enough models who couldn't make it in America. They would ornament the local hot spots looking dizzy and hungry and tragic. Especially the male models. On the street one day I met a man from the States—a baseball player. He said he hadn't been able to get picked up by an American major-league team but here he was treated like royalty. I knew how he felt. In the rest of Asia, they didn't even know I existed . . . not at that time . . . so I have to admit being in Taipei was kind of fun.

≈

My junior year, I showed up for my first day of boarding school wearing baggy 501s, a biker jacket, and a large skinning knife on my belt. No one knew what to do with me. I didn't fit the mold.

For me, boarding school might as well have been Mars. I had always been treated like a responsible adult by my parents, and prior to the eleventh grade, I had already been living on my own. I was used to a lot of freedom. Needless to say, dorm life was hell for me . . . but creatively, Interlochen was fantastic. The instruction I received was top-notch. I was stimulated and pushed to excel. I flourished artistically.

I had won a vocal scholarship, so that was certainly a field of interest for me, but I had also chosen to major in visual arts and minor in drama and dance. This worried the dean. The administration at Interlochen preferred students to stick to one major field of study so they could devote themselves to that skill full-time. Since students routinely devoted themselves to six to eight hours of academics a day and up to five hours of rehearsal, there really wasn't time for "unfocused" exploration. But the administration also knew that artistically, I had an irrepressible appetite. They let me go for it. I skipped lunch to take sculpture. I danced ballet and modern every morning. And my voice teacher taught me to work my voice the way I'd seen my father work the horses: gently but firmly, building on my strengths while building up my weaknesses. I couldn't read music, so I listened very carefully. I learned to sing arias by ear. And I discovered a falsetto I never knew I had. I was doing what I loved.

I was also doing what I knew. For extra cash and just to get out, I got a gig at a local piano bar in Traverse City with the piano player who played accompaniment for the Interlochen dance classes, Charles Sampson. He taught me a lot about jazz standards and blues. He also showed me that a career in music could be supplemented by sidelining as a pool shark. It wasn't long before I was summoned to the dean of students' office. An underage student, singing alone in a bar with a faculty member? Well . . . it just wasn't done. But I explained to the dean that Charles wasn't my type and not to worry: I had been singing in bars longer than he'd been a dean. He raised an eyebrow but went pretty easy on me. In retrospect, I must have seemed like some wild creature from, well . . . Alaska.

Creatively, Interlochen was pivotal. The level of excellence and self-motivation at the school changed my perspective completely. For the first time I was around kids who were very young, very talented, and highly motivated. That experience taught me to take my gifts and talents very seriously and to pursue excellence. My creativity went from hobby to all that mattered.

Socially, I was a bit of a black sheep. I was neither the star soprano, nor the most promising sculptor, nor the premier dancer. Heck, I was not even the flavor of the week! There were three girls to every boy at Interlochen. I couldn't get a guy to look at me if I set myself on fire! And I wasn't a part of the traditional after-dinner ritual—at least among the dance majors: the flushing of the toilets. Anorexia is much less noisy than bulimia, but no less obvious.

In my dorm room, late at night, I had begun to write my first songs—"Don't" and "Who Will Save Your Soul?" Writing songs began to excite me more than all the other art forms I was taking classes in. I began to envision my future, not as a sculptor or as an opera singer or as a farm girl, but as a songwriter.

Being poor makes you aware of how terribly dependent you are on others to survive. You're dependent on the social services department and the counselor's mood. She's what stands between you and your next meal. You're dependent on the doctor at the clinic: Does he care about your kidneys? Or is he biding his time until a better job comes along? You're dependent on the man who's paying you under the table. If you don't do everything he wants, will he really turn you in?

But you're also dependent on the kindness of others. As

many times as I've been disappointed, I've been
amazed at the compassion of strangers. That's
what makes it possible to believe . . . that you
will make it another day . . . that somebody
cares . . . that you can come through even this
untouched by hate, nourished by an ultimate
goodness.

It is hard to revisit how lonely and sad I became without my mother near me every day. Holidays together were not enough. Though we painted them with a desperately happy mood, there was sadness beneath the surface. Being with Mom when I could was like heaven. She was so calm and magical. Most important, she was my mom. She held me. She told me things would be okay. She made me believe I'd be okay.

My mom was never absent from our lives. We talked on the phone as much as our budget allowed. We lived with her some summers and holidays, and eventually entire school years when I was in my teens. But day to day, month to month, life without her was very difficult.

I loved my father dearly. I would have hated not to be with him, either. Divorce is hard that way. But life with my dad was dark and hard for a long time.

So much of the time after the divorce I felt lonely. A deep, deep sorrow. It was as though all the tenderness had left my life. My dad never held me or played with me. Everything was strained and solitary. I often had the feeling sorrow would smother me entirely. It undermined every triumph and lurked beneath every success. I began writing my sorrow to get it outside of my own skin. I began writing so I wouldn't drown in vague, unvoiced pain. I wrote more than I spoke. Finally, I lost confidence and became withdrawn.

I remember I called my mom once and told her that I didn't think I could make it with my dad much longer. I no longer felt happy—ever. I felt heavy and unlike myself. I told her I was worried I would never be the way I had been, that I would forget the happy, outgoing person I used to be. I felt like I was breaking.

My mother spoke to me in a very serious voice. She told me to listen carefully. She said there was a place in me that could never be broken. Then she asked me to shut my eyes and look inside myself until I sensed that place. She reminded me that she was doing everything she could to get us back with her and that it wouldn't be long until she could afford a house where we could all live. Until then, she told me to know how strong I was, to spend time remembering the way I used to be, and never give in. Change was coming. Until it did, she assured me, I'd be fine. I'd hang on. She asked me if I understood.

I felt proud to know that she felt I was strong. I felt proud that she believed there was some place within me where I was always wise and untouchable and unbreakable. I would trust that. *Yes,* I told her. *I understand.*

As it turned out, that winter I ended up moving to Hawaii with my aunt, then to Anchorage, where I lived with Nedra until I turned sixteen. Then I moved out on my own.

That summer was the last time I really lived with my dad.

Jacque's Birthday

Today is August 17. It is my best friend's birthday. It is the first birthday to pass since she died. She was a Leo.

Her family is not all together today but scattered across the country. I talked to her son, Sean. His voice sounded a lot like mine, heavy and thoughtful.

Some days it's hard to believe in anything. Some days it seems that the heart has been sucked out of the entire world, so that everything seems cold and absurd and perhaps pointless. I feel like a child who knows less than nothing.

Tonight I could barely face people. I had to force myself to walk on-stage. I did not want to be applauded or heckled or even looked at. I wanted to sit at Jacque's feet again and have her pet my hair and make me feel safe. Nobody could make me feel safer than Jacque. She was so wise and smart, and she loved people as much as she loved God. She even loved me when I couldn't love myself. And she was always proud of me, even when I disappointed myself.

This is how I want to love.

This is how I want to be loved.

I feel her still, of course. But I miss her physically. Being held. Being listened to. I miss rubbing her feet and watching her eat Skittles and jelly beans instead of breakfast.

If she were here, there is so much I'd tell her. I'd tell her that at times I have been hurt and disappointed and embarrassed by myself. I would tell her that I am learning not to be. And I would tell her that I am making her birthday wish come true: I am happy. I'm maturing. I'm becoming a woman I know she'd be proud of.

After the divorce, my mom won a scholarship to Pilchuk, a famous art-glass school in Washington. Then she started her own glass studio and gallery. When I was nine and my brothers and I stayed with her, we lived in the building that housed the studio, in the attached apartment. The house and gallery were in Spenard, a funky section of Anchorage.

The structure stood out in stark contrast to its surroundings. Then again, it would stand out in pretty much any surroundings. It was painted pink with white trim and had a neon sign that read VITRICS GALLERY. Downstairs was Nedra's bedroom and workshop. There she assembled huge stained-glass panels for clients. There was also a booth where she sandblasted thick slabs of glass, etching them with her own distinctive designs. For presents and holidays and really anytime we wanted, she allowed us into the studio to solder or sandblast our own creations.

I made one friend my age. She was Athabascan, with long, silky black hair and one lazy eye. I visited her often in the rust-colored apartment building next door. One day I got there when she was "cooking." I watched carefully as she mixed vodka with orange juice, then poured the mixture into Popsicle molds to freeze. She ate the pops until they ran out: for breakfast . . . snacks . . . then she made another batch. I asked her if her parents knew that she was using their booze; she said probably. They're the ones who showed her how to make the pops. They made them all the time.

My friend was a little strange and a little slow, and in hindsight, I think she may have had fetal alcohol syndrome.

Where are the friends I made in Anchorage now?

Well, I've seen Amir. Amir was a great friend—funny and loyal. Just walking the school halls with him was entertainment. Then one day he told me he didn't want me hanging around with my gay friends, whom he referred to as "fags." I argued the point but he wouldn't hear of it. To Amir, "that crap just wasn't natural." We drifted apart. Years later I ran into him in San Diego. He was with his boyfriend. (This is when I wrote "Pieces of You.")

As for the rest of them, Vinnie got into dealing and dropped out of school. Dani, Amir's sister, ended up in a juvenile hall for some gang-related crime, and Buffy, Amir's brother, was in a correctional center, last I knew. Cara stayed straight. She never did drugs, drank, or skipped classes. She did everything she could to stay focused and sane, despite her disadvantages. She won an American Indian scholarship and went to college in Kansas. As far as I know, Cara is now working to help the Aleut nation transition from near extinction into the twenty-first century.

Growing up with my mom was very inspiring. No matter how poor we were, she always had a way of making us feel safe and okay. She always impressed upon us that an obstacle was a creative opportunity in disguise, and with the right attitude and some creative thinking, we could turn it to our advantage. She also protected our sense of wonder and awe and gratitude for the world.

Creativity goes beyond being a Picasso; it spills into all areas of life. A sense of curiosity and a bit of imagination help develop problem-solving skills that you can apply personally and professionally. That's why I believe so strongly in arts in the schools—and certainly at home. Mom continually reminded us that we had no limits. She held poetry workshops with us and turned me on to cool music like Edith Piaf and Bulgarian choirs. She also involved us in debates and dialogues on everything from our own happiness to politics and literature. We had plenty to say—and learned to be not just opinionated but thoughtful and articulate.

Our surroundings were sometimes gray, but with Nedra there was always a sense that anything was possible—which, each day, again and again, has only proven to be true. Much of the person I've become has been nurtured by her quiet way of teaching.

～

It's strange to think that from age twenty on, I've lived almost continually in hotels around the world. Hotels and tour buses.

～

Columbus

I walked out of my hotel with a friend hoping to find a nice quiet place for breakfast. The first thing I see are the same three people as the night before, still waiting for an autograph. We could tell they'd been up all night. They were wearing the same clothes and were bleary-eyed and stubbly. They'd been haunting the hotel for thirteen hours, not wanting to miss catching me again.

Just last night, after my show, I had stopped and signed one autograph for each of them: no names so they could sell them if they wanted. Personalized autographs, I have learned, have limited prospects on the secondary market. I look the group over. That's the same guy all right, wearing the same orange sweatshirt. Last night he presented me with a folder full of pictures. He asked me to sign another for his sister, Annette. Since I had already signed an autograph for each of them, I said no. I wanted to go to bed. But there he was again, for Annette, and since I was feeling rested, I obliged. I was still writing when a young woman approached.

"To whom?" I asked her.

"Uh, no name. Just sign it, okay?"

I told her I had to have a name. Usually a pro will hassle you, gripe if you refuse to "just sign," then—if you really insist—give you some generic name like Joe. The secondary market is bound to attract a few Joes. But this girl did neither. She just grew sullen and let the photograph of me drop to her side. I remembered signing one for her the night before, so I just moved on.

My friend and I strolled a few blocks then dropped in to a cute café. We took our time, savoring the time off and the waffles. We were nearly to the hotel when we encountered them—the same three people still clutching their photographs.

The girl came up to me angrily. "Have you forgotten?" she pressed. She was pretty and petite.

"Sorry?"

"You know. Have you forgotten what it's like? This autograph will make money for me and my daughter. Have you forgotten what it's like to be poor, or what?"

"No," I answered, somewhat stunned. "I haven't forgotten what it's like to be poor." As I reached for one of her pictures, I asked her: "What do you get for these anyway?" She said some are worth up to $150.

I found the whole thing disturbing. Yes, I had been poor, but I didn't stalk people for autographs and expect them to oblige out of some sense of duty.

But who's to judge another human being? I wanted to be fair. All I knew was that the whole interaction with this girl made me feel terrible. Would I feel better if I signed every photograph someone shoves my way? Would I be cleansed if I signed all sixty the boy in the orange sweatshirt had in his folder? And these were two people on one morning. What if there were a hundred people a day with ten pictures each? What is enough? Was I to believe that my scrawl on a piece of paper would make or break another human being?

The girl thanked me and turned away with her second autograph, but the guy in the orange shirt followed me down the street, calling behind me: "Just one more! Come on! It takes no time! You can put a name on it if you want!"

By this time my cheeks were flushed and hot. I felt embarrassed. I had already signed two for him and I was anxious to get back to my hotel. People were coming out of stores and starting to stare. Finally, my friend put himself between me and the man, blocking his way as he tried to grab my coat sleeve.

But as the doors shut behind us, I could still hear him calling: "Aw, come on! Just one more! Jewel! This is the price you pay for fame."

❧

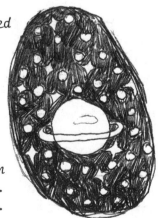

When I was on the road, I used to speak with Jacque on the phone every night, just to connect with something familiar. You begin to feel like you're an astronaut on the road, you're in outer space and there's no oxygen and it's cold and nothing can touch you in your space suit. She was always so comforting.

❧

NYC, Autumn

For two consecutive days I have been completely alone. Well, as alone as someone can be in New York City. Sometimes I think it can be the most lonesome city in the world, but for now I'm enjoying the time to be still.

I was just too tired to go home. The five-hour flight to California seemed unthinkably exhausting . . . like walking cross-country. I stand on the corner of Fifty-seventh and Broadway and stare at my reflection in a store window. I look and feel like I've been frozen and thawed too many times. My mind feels muddled and anxious from not sleeping and I'd swear that the force of gravity has increased tenfold. But still, how lovely it is to be alone.

No one I work with is in the hotel or even in the city, so I get to be on my own. Today I am a normal, anonymous person who gets to sleep in, then venture out to buy normal things at a drugstore like a comb and hair clips and toothpaste and bottled water. I get to sit in a café at the table by the window and watch people's lives unfold, briefly, until they pay their checks and take their intense discussions and air kisses beyond my range of vision. I get to walk into the park and lie on my back and stare at the leaves and blue sky for hours and let my mind do what it was made to do, imagine and absorb and think and wander and suppose and speculate and watch. With no agenda. Just be.

❧

Underneath a starry sky
You're just a stranger
Tut, tut, ain't it embarrassing
yesterday's lover

❧

I have had chronic kidney and bladder infections since I was sixteen years old. Often I was unable to afford the expensive antibiotics. I tried every natural remedy I could. When I'd get an infection I'd try to fight it off by drinking gallons of unsweetened cranberry and pomegranate juice. To this day the smell of pomegranate juice is enough to make me feel queasy.

Once, when I was too short on cash to even do the juice routine, I let an infection go. I suffered through the pain and hoped it would just go away. But it didn't. Soon I was doubled over, throwing up. Nedra knew that once the kidneys stopped working properly, it was possible to develop blood toxicity and perhaps even die. Though we were new to Southern California and didn't know our way around, Nedra didn't waste any time: she got me into my little car and drove me into town, where we'd seen a hospital. But nearly as soon as Nedra went in, she came storming back out, mad as hell. The doctors there wouldn't see me without insurance or payment in hand. By now I was in the passenger seat, sweating and throwing up. She held me. We were trying to avoid going to the emergency room because we couldn't pay the steep fees. So we went to another doctor's office. Then another. By this point I was crying and dry-heaving and nearly as overwhelmed by embarrassment and shame as I was by the illness. Nedra was now in tears. We had no choice. We went back to the hospital and signed into the emergency room.

A few minutes later I had been diagnosed and a very nice doctor was writing a prescription for me. I asked him if maybe he could fix me up with some samples instead, because I didn't have the money for the medicine. He understood. He recommended that I set up an appointment with a friend of his who was a specialist. The specialist would help me out if I could get myself covered by Medicaid.

I did my part. I stood in the long lines in social services buildings. I cooperated with the counselors. I submitted to ongoing income checks to make sure I wasn't hiding a wad of cash . . . where? In my empty caviar tins? But in the end the specialist wasn't able to do much. I was simply prone to this type of sickness and we hoped I'd grow out of it.

The economy was booming, yet I was a "throwaway" person. No one cared about my health because no one had to. Over time, by working with nutritionists and herbalists and other healers, my situation has improved. I get sick only six or eight times a year now.

❧

Living underground beneath a junkyard didn't keep Stinky from entertaining visitors. If you wanted to see him, all you had to do was drive to the end of a dirt road and park among the wrecked cars and pillaged washing machines and scrap metal. Then get out of your car and yell, "Stinky!" as loud as you could.

The story was that Stinky had moved to Alaska sometime during the cold war and subsequent bomb-shelter craze. He was so sure that the Russians wouldn't bomb Alaska that he moved from who-knows-where. Still, he built himself a home underground. Somehow, he ran electricity to his place. I heard there were lightbulbs strung from the ceiling. It was probably quite homey.

Too bad he didn't have a doorbell. You'd have to yell very loud for Stinky to hear you. Then you'd notice a refrigerator on its back slowly open up like a coffin and up would come Stinky, step by step, until finally he'd just walk out of the refrigerator and come to see what you wanted. Other times he'd just peer out of the fridge, so all you could see was the top of his head, like a gopher peeking out of its hole.

I have a house now with things in it I seldom see. Clothes I never wear because they don't travel well. What I see of my life fits into my two suitcases. A third is for my pillow and my down comforter. I got so tired of never sleeping on my own bedding I finally got wise and started traveling with it.
   Home *is* where I'm headed.

The tour started in Australia, which is lovely for many reasons—the main one being that February is like July, weather-wise. So no freezing for Jewel. For her it's constant summer.

❧

Being poor reveals a vulnerability that can make you feel weak. It is not unusual for a poor woman to discover that certain "duties" have been added to her job description by a horny, needy, or power-mad boss. I was no exception. Would I care to go out to dinner one night after work? I was thrilled for any opportunity to go out to a nice dinner, one with white tablecloths. So when I, at age eighteen, was invited out for a meal by the man who paid me next to nothing to answer his phones, I decided to go ahead and do it.

I was soaking up the ambience of the restaurant and chowing down when my boss mentioned that it must be obvious that he was interested in me. I didn't know what to say. What was he thinking?! Was he joking? I politely but clearly said that a relationship with him just wasn't an interest for me, and besides, the fact that he was twice my age *and* my boss seemed to doom any prospects of romance between us. He seemed to agree. We finished our meals hastily and I drove myself home.

A week later, on the day the rent was due, I went to work eager to get my paycheck. But when the checks were handed out, there didn't seem to be one for me. I needed that paycheck for my rent. I went into the boss's office and asked for my check.

It was the first time I had seen him, really, since dinner. Clearly, something in him had hardened since we revealed our feelings over previously frozen "freshly made" apple pie. He stared at me coldly and told me in a flat tone that I wouldn't be getting my check today. I panicked. I really needed that money, I explained. He said it would be impossible. I had to have it or I'd be out on the street, I insisted. He said I might as well leave.

I went home in a panic. Did I bring this upon myself? I was humiliated. Nedra was always there for me. How could I tell her I didn't have my half of the rent? It took all my courage to confess what had happened—and when I did, she was livid, but not with me.

She marched me straight back to the office and burst through the boss's door.

"You wanted to sleep with my daughter?" she demanded.

My boss went white.

"You wanted to sleep with my daughter?" Nedra looked him in the eye. "Well, you may not have slept with her but you just screwed her pretty good!"

We got our check.

Nedra had suggested before that I might move into my van and now I began to seriously consider it. I couldn't stand the idea of getting another job that didn't have anything to do with my dream. Nedra pointed out that if I didn't have to come up with the rent every month it would free me to sing full-time.

It was a shocking idea. A shocking, amazing, liberating idea. And as soon as Nedra verbalized it, I felt deeply relieved. Maybe I could get a weekly gig somewhere. This would free me up to sing and write and figure myself out without worrying about rent. However, I was still tentative. Until Nedra said, "Let's both do it." That was when everything started to change.

Fear had kept a stranglehold on my life for so long, I had begun to feel like a victim of circumstance. A puppet with no will of my own. But now that I had made the leap into the unknown, of my own volition, I began to feel that perhaps the unknown wasn't so scary after all. Maybe, I thought, life wasn't something that happened to me. Maybe, just maybe, it was something I created, like an intricate weaving, from the threads of my own perceptions. And if that were true, couldn't I snap the thread of fear that had bound my heart? Couldn't I create a brighter pattern for the life that was unfolding before me?

Living in my van, I was able to take a clear look at my life. All of my focus had been on what I lacked, how ill I was, how I suffered. Virtually none of my energy had been spent imagining how else it could be. I began to require of myself a new way of being in my life. I realized that if all I focused on was limitation, then limit was what I would create. There was a whole world of possibility I had left unexplored, and now I wanted to explore it. It was like a switch in my head. For instance, as I'd drive down the road, if I began to panic, worrying that everything was wrong—I might get sick, I might never make it singing—I would simply flip the switch and say, "It's all okay. I'm doing good shows. I'm getting sick less frequently."

It wasn't long before I began to feel excitement instead of dread. I'd flip the switch again and again, as often as I had to, sometimes several times a day, sometimes every five minutes, until gradually I retrained my thought process and restructured how I perceived myself and the influence I held over my world. More than awards, more than money, more than record sales, this is what I consider my success. And amazingly, it has worked. By any social worker's standards, I was homeless. But for the first time in a long time I felt my life was on its true course. I was participating in my own miracle.

CHAPTER *5*

I woke early this morning, tiptoed past the band still sleeping in their bunks, took my seat next to the driver, and watched the sun burn a hole through—where are we?—Ohio.

Well, when you go to bed at four A.M., one o'clock in the afternoon is early . . .

Tennessee, December

There is ice on all the trees. Limbs encased in transparent sleeves that glitter like the bejeweled treasures that Chinese princesses wear in fairy tales. Uncannily silent. A vacuous silence that is caused by bitter cold. Only hollow brittle sounds tinker and clatter when a breeze blows.

No bright voices fill the streets. The children are all inside huddled under blankets. In the morning, they will walk from the warmth of their houses into a new kind of world, a world where ice drapes mailboxes and street signs and entire cars in crystal tombs. Buses with chains on each wheel will pick them up and take them to school, where they struggle to resist the irresistible urge to stick their pink tongues against the smooth, ice-encased flagpole and monkey bars. The chain links of a swing set sparkle like strings of diamonds. The kids will dance briefly in the school yard, restless from weeks of cold, until their teachers cut their playtime short and gather them in the library to listen to stories read by a blasé librarian or nervous soccer coach.

Ice-storm warnings for eastern Tennessee. Small white houses with cozy lights and rough-cheeked spectators peeking out of windows and calling the neighbors.

Did you hear? The bridges are running slow.

Well, can I drive? I have a hair appointment at Mary's shop. Uh-huh. Just moving slow? Then I'll take my chances. Call me in the car.

Most of the people born in Tennessee know how to drive in these conditions. Trouble is, this town is filled with transplants who are inexperienced ice-drivers. You don't see this kind of chaos in Alaska. No canceled school or workdays. Not many accidents, either, except for the drunks who happen into hazardous territory trying to make it home on ice. But in Alaska I've never seen ice storms like this. There is ice, of course . . . lots of black, unfriendly ice. But here it is magical somehow, a swift cold front that causes the lakes to steam like hot springs and leaves every streetlamp and blade of grass encased in a clear sheath of ice.

We drive two hours from Talbott to Oak Ridge. I sit quietly staring out my window. Icicles have formed on the mirror outside. They match my mood. I feel solitary and deeply quiet. A cold kind of suspended poetry. Peaceful.

༄

It is a moment most of us experience—the first time we realize our-selves as an individual, conscious and aware. For me it was at the foot of a staircase, about age three. My mother called my name, and for some reason everything focused or snapped and I connected the name my mother was calling out to me, to myself.

Periodically, over the years, at certain moments, I'd become strangely aware of myself again. I'd lay on the bed and see how much farther my feet were from me and marvel that my body was growing around me. Or notice that I was becoming more dexterous, or skilled. Each time this would happen, what I loved most was that I was aware of myself *inside* myself. That I was a consciousness that inhabited this space, this body, a spirit that permeated my body, giving it animation.

I learned to keep an ear turned always inward, to track and dialogue with that inner voice. I often found the voice within me possessed a wis-dom or peace beyond my years or experience. During stressful times I would take great solace retreating inside. I felt things would be okay.

From a young age my mother encouraged me to turn my ear to the subtle voice that was inside me. Without her encouragement I'm sure I would have become numb to it.

There were times when I lost touch with the voice. It felt like losing the compass by which I have always navigated. There have been times when I have lost trust and faith in my own intuition and tumbled around aimlessly, like a ship tossed against the rocks of other people's opinions and criticisms. Writing has helped me immeasurably. What I feel most deeply surfaces when I write. It is a very tangible way to see what inwardly has no form.

I sit in silence each day for one to two hours, not to pray or medi-tate, though it may be like that. It is to sit in communion with myself, to dialogue inwardly, to dream new dreams, to redream old ones. To up-date old habits or thought processes that no longer serve me, to contemplate the source and the wonder of all things.

I'm getting better at hearing my voice. I'm learning that the more I make decisions from my gut, regardless of statistics or popular opinion, the happier I am with the outcome . . . the more the outcome looks like who I am, not what I feel obligated to be.

❧

Brussels

Time is a loop, not a line. I am a child and I am ancient, the world flying around my ears. And time can be heard. It is the cumulative sound of sighs and broken limbs and untouched hearts and yellow grass. It is the hummmmm of empty bars and the cool laugh of the seductress who hangs on to elbows with too stiff a hand and eyes that linger, not out of hunger or love, but simply because they covet.

Time passes in waltz time, slipping between the steel strings played by a virtuoso or by a boy in the Ozarks. It tangos with honeybees and flirts with blue eye shadow. Time has a noise. It is the squeak of rosy cheeks pressed on cold window panes while outside the rain resuscitates dry leaves and floods basements with indifference. Ants and automobiles swimming on their backs.

Small hands will scribble and lend themselves to the noise. A woman will add to the refrain, thinking as she stares in the mirror, *I wear my age well. My wrinkles are handsome to me.* It is a song she'll sing to herself.

I am made dizzy by how glorious and noisy time makes itself. I turn my ear to it often—on airplanes, on crowded streets, on quiet horseback rides.

❧

It was my eighth-grade year and I was at a new school in Anchorage. I had spent the first half of the year in Hawaii living with my aunt and uncle who were a captain and a lieutenant in the Marine Corps. It turned out to be a difficult arrangement. Home life was like boot camp—strict and unhappy—and school life was insane. The native Hawaiian kids resented the whites. The culture shock of the whole experience was very disturbing, and by the time I made it back to Alaska to live with my mom, I was a pretty confused kid. All I wanted was to fit in.

I tried all sorts of things to fit in. I curled my hair, applied makeup, even briefly changed my name to Sandy, something less unusual. It became apparent quite quickly that none of this made me feel more normal. What is normal, anyway? Did anyone feel normal? Did even the most stoned stoner or muscle-bound jock or prettiest, most popular girl feel normal? Probably not. Everyone was insecure, wanted to be told they were beautiful or talented, just like I did.

I realized that when I compared myself to others I lost who I was. It seemed my vitality faded the more I focused on how others were . . . what they did and thought. I began tempering my uniqueness and homogenizing my spark. This felt alien to me. My mom was an artist and had always encouraged me to experiment with the way I dressed, sang, drew, and wrote. It felt so much better not to worry about looking cool or fitting in and to express myself instead. When I did that, I found my taste in clothes and music changed often, as they still do today. My writing styles began to branch out and I began to create who I was, who I wanted to be.

The idea that fame transforms all problems is true financially and in many other ways, but no glass slipper can quiet the ghosts that haunt a psyche.

❧

Jacque

What shall I say of her?

I live without her now. My dear, sweet Jacque. I cry even now, writing of her. Though her absence is still unthinkable, it is easier now, more than a year after her death.

And what shall I say of her death? No death is kind, I suppose, but some are more cruel than others and cancer is one of the most unkind. It is cruel. It hurt her. It hurt her slowly, intensely, and for a long time. That is what pains me the most.

After she died, I cried all the time. My eyes would well suddenly, in the middle of conversations. I had no idea my heart was capable of such heavy, thick sorrow. Black sorrow. Silent sorrow, like a ship lost at sea on a starless, wordless night.

I live without her now. Without her words and her laughter. Without hope that I will ever sit with her again, feeling her pet my hair, listening to her speak to me of things that soothed me in the deepest ways.

Grief is such a painful yet intangible thing. It sweeps over the soul with ferocity but informs us of nothing—just loss. I miss her. More than anything, I miss her touch.

Right now I am sitting beneath an oak tree, in a sunny spot, writing about you for my book. I am crying. Do you hear me? Do you feel it? Do you feel the ache and the longing? No malice—just ache, deep ache.

I wish for things I cannot have. Your blue eyes. Your pink toenails. Your tangled black hair. Where does love go when it can't find a home?

I love you I love you I love you.

❧

When I was young, I used to steal a fair amount.

In eighth grade, we moved to Anchorage. Big city. The kids there said I smelled like horse manure. But a very pretty, popular girl befriended me—or maybe she "took me on," like a charity project. Anyway, she was nice enough to invite me to her house frequently. It was like inviting a starving person to a banquet.

My friend had beautiful things . . . and lots of them. Duran Duran *making music*

two other young performers on a local Anchorage

Me, my brothers, and

radio show

Hotel gig, age 7

Gig at the University of

Anchorage, Alaska, age 13 or 14

Part of the act was me yodeling—which I enjoyed.

The part that always embarrassed me was the lyrics—"Moonbeams were shining as I kissed him there." To

further embarrass me, my dad would make a large

kissing noise off-mike—so I could hear—which usually sent me into a spasm of rolling eyeballs.

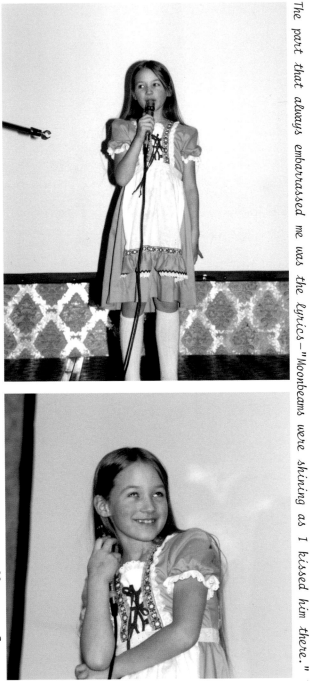

A bar for veterans called Am Vets

KBBI concert on the lawn

Homer, Alaska

Same KBBI gig, different (and colder) year

Poltz and I during the "Down So Long" video shoot

Rehearsals for Radio Shack gig, '00

Bar in D.C., '95

"Who Will Save Your Soul" in the studio for my first album

In the studio with Juan Patino

Mall in Melbourne

Dollhouse in San Francisco

Mom, Rome

My brother Atz, London

Jacque, Manitoba

Mom, Greece

Just the girls: Backstage at Lilith Fair (left to right) Sarah McLachlan, Yungchen Lhamo, me, Sheryl Crow

Emmylou Harris and me, Lilith Fair

Flea and me in the studio with Chris Shaw, Bearsville, New York

Niagara Falls

Paris

On assignment for MTV

Rock the Vote, Democratic Convention

Glamour of the road, Somewhere, USA

On a canal in Venice

After a gig, Dublin

My band and me waiting for a train in Osaka, Japan

Brady Blade, drummer extraordinaire

The band (left to right), Windsor Castle: Doug Pettibone a.k.a. Big Head, Steve George a.k.a. UD (Union Delegate), Steve Poltz a.k.a. Polio Boy (yes, 'cause he's skinny), Brady Blade a.k.a. Oscar, me a.k.a. Governor, Tony Hall a.k.a. Felix. I LOVE these guys!

Doug, Poltz, and me clowning in Atlantic City

My 1st Grammy

My brother Atz on harmonica, Amsterdam

"Down So Long" video shoot

San Diego

Los Angeles

Waiting to shoot the "Foolish Games" video

and Easy-E tapes. Curling irons. Cool clothes. Jewelry. Everything I thought I needed to feel better about myself. It started one day with a necklace. I thought, *She'll never miss this, she'll think she lost it.* But it didn't stop there.

One day, while my friend wasn't home, I took a ridiculous amount of stuff. Clothes. Hair clips. Cosmetics. Music and a boom box to play it on. The whole lot. It was as if a mover had stopped by and packed up my friend's entire room. I even went to the kitchen for garbage bags to cart it all off.

It was obvious who had done it. My friend's mother said it was as if I wanted to get caught. She and her daughter were very nice about it, which made me feel worse. Nobody seemed angry, they just pitied me. They called my mom and I returned the stuff. It took me years to realize stealing was a manifestation of my lack of faith in myself. If I really knew who I was, I wouldn't be so needy. I wouldn't have an empty space inside, or the inclination to fill that void with everything I could get my paws on. If I had faith and pride, I wouldn't covet what someone else had. I would recognize and take pride in the many gifts I'd been given.

Stealing showed a direct lack of faith in God. After all, if I believed in God and that God took care of me, why would I steal? It was a double standard. I wanted to be bigger than that.

So I stopped. And although I still longed for stuff, I came to understand that it was okay to want. I already had everything I needed to get everything I wanted. All I had to do was get my act together and start valuing myself.

I began to make a game out of it. If there was something I needed, I'd trust that it would come. I'd get excited, picture it, fantasize about it. Every time, what I visualized came to me. One day, when I was living in my car, I needed five dollars for dinner. The day was almost over and it seemed like I was going to be disappointed. Then, all of a sudden, these skater kids came over.

"Hey, you play that guitar?" they called to me.

"Yeah."

"Then sing for us."

I considered my options. "What'll you give me?"

They dug around in their pockets and gave me five dollars in change, exactly. My prayer had been answered. Small miracles, but they built my faith and have led me to even greater ones.

❧

It is easy to look at my life now and say it was my destiny to become a musician. I was born and bred into it, but the truth is there are many things I could have become. I could be a waitress, a receptionist, a busker, or any of the things I have been in my life. I could be a poor kid who sings a little. I've got that gig down pat. The point is, there is no grand design that limits what we can be or guarantees it coming.

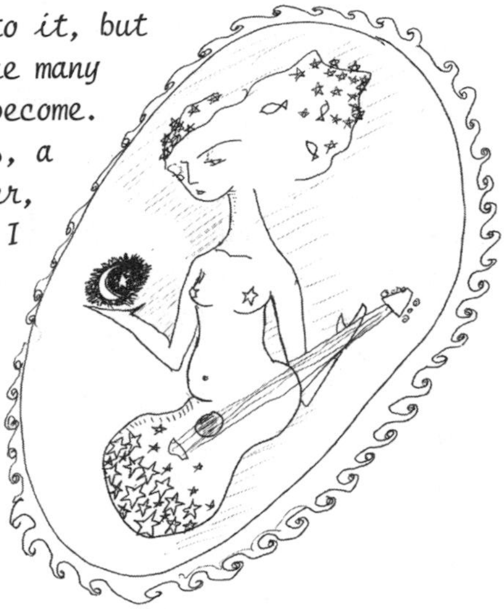

❧

After I graduated from high school, I lived in Boulder, Colorado, with some school friends. I applied for a position as a nanny in the home of a very nice family.

I had no car to get to the interview, so a friend dropped me off. The father of the family offered very kindly to drive me home. We talked casually in the car, and when I got out, he said he'd be in touch about whether I would be hired. He called two nights later and invited me to dinner, to discuss, I assumed, the details of my employment.

At dinner he seemed curiously nervous and awkward. It wasn't long before I discovered why. In the middle of our conversation he clumsily blurted out that he'd "never done anything like this before."

"Like what?" I asked, perplexed.

"Had an affair," he offered, as if this statement referred to a prediscussed arrangement.

I was floored. It dawned on me then that we were eating at a restaurant in a very nice hotel. I put down the shrimp I was eating and said very clearly, "I came to your house looking for a job and nothing else. I need the work."

He asked how much money I needed. I told him I needed $1,500 to leave Colorado and get to San Diego, where my mom was. He was calm and confident by now. He had that much in his pocket, he reported. I asked him to drive me home.

We did not finish dinner. We didn't even speak on the way home. Nor did I say a word when I shut the car door and walked into my apartment, leaving him alone in his car to drive back to his wife and babies. But I won't lie. I thought about it.

～

Kuala Lumpur

I am staring out my window from the twenty-fourth floor. Below me are a small cluster of luscious trees. They look like they have turned their backs on the metal and mopeds of the city, which has been rising up around them in the last hundred years.

Even from up here, I can see the bright yellow backs of birds that dart from limb to bough. I can't get over the green. It is shockingly vivid and moist. The leaves seem plump and swollen with the humidity that is constant in the east. In the distance are the famed silhouettes of the craggy Asian hills, which etch themselves into the same hazy skyline that has been the subject of artists and poets for centuries. I am just passing through.

To my right stands the tallest building in the world. It is mostly empty now due to the Asian market crash. Only a few windows are lit, leaving the rest to look like missing teeth in a rich man's smile. Being here, close enough to see the weight that burdens each person, I can feel the depth to which poverty bites their hearts.

Driving in from the airport I saw small plots of land where a few cattle grazed in dull circles amid the bushes and weeds, just outside the small shack that was someone's house. A tin roof and only three walls of plywood. Inside I could see colorful decorations and a large picture of Jesus with a yellow halo. Paper plates that had been colored with pieces of bright tissue paper glued to them in cheerful bursts. One room. No frills. Conveniently close to a dilapidated barn that housed six more cattle and one scrawny goat.

In the yard, a man with no shirt was carrying a bucket to the animals. The animals had more meat on their bones than the man who fed them. Here the cows could be worth more than their keeper; they are his wealth.

In the city it is hustle and bustle as usual. Indonesia is worse off, my driver tells me. At least no one in Kuala Lumpur is cutting anyone's head off and parading it down the street, he said, referring to the latest news. I smile politely. The advantages of people's lives are relative.

The sun bleeds like a hole pierced in the sky. The clouds leave chalky smears that hold less and less light. Soon it will be dark. Then the windows of the very tall building will look as if they are floating randomly in the night sky, like blank flags that belong to a country no one owns.

✧

My childhood prepared me in nearly every way to be a musician and performer. From the time I could stand on a stage, everything was about the gig: how to handle the club owners and the crowds . . . how to write and perform music that created a sense of connection when you sang it . . . and most of all, how to be professional. Even if you were a gawky grade-school kid. No excuses.

As arduous as our relationship was, music provided my father and me with a home for our love for each other . . . and some much-needed common ground. And I worked myself very hard to earn his respect and admiration. We were being paid to do a show—not to sulk or pout, he told me.

The discipline, work ethic, and professionalism I learned from him have contributed immeasurably to my life today. Work hard. Read the crowd. Play your heart out every night. Never give anything less. And always take pride in the show.

❧

Now people react to me in lots of different ways. Some get tongue-tied. Some cry. Others will cross a crowded room just to say, "Hey—you're not so great. You think you're big just because you're on magazine covers. But that doesn't make you special."

To which I think, "Well, hell— I could have told you that!"

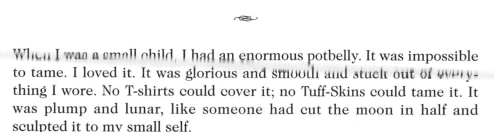

❧

When I was a small child, I had an enormous potbelly. It was impossible to tame. I loved it. It was glorious and smooth and stuck out of everything I wore. No T-shirts could cover it; no Tuff-Skins could tame it. It was plump and lunar, like someone had cut the moon in half and sculpted it to my small self.

I was still quite young when I began to catch on that a belly wasn't something to be desired; it was something to be ashamed of. Girls wanted breasts; to wear earrings; to cram their feet into uncomfortable shoes. Potbellies were not in demand. They were not even considered attractive, and everything I saw, heard, and read reminded me that being attractive was the point of it all.

❧

I am asked often if I think my looks help me in my job. I would have to say yes. Looks are a big deal in my line of work. All the time I see women in my profession work as hard, if not harder, on making their bodies perfect as they do on developing their craft. And I understand why. It is a very vulnerable feeling, to say the least, to stand before the entire free world knowing that people will comment, in print or in the privacy of their own homes, that, gee, her hair doesn't look great, or look, she has a lumpy ass, or hey, doesn't she look too thin or too fat? There is a nagging sense of fear in every woman, famous or not, who suspects that the world will forget her as soon as someone younger or more fantastic-looking comes along. And the turnover is high.

I've had to decide not to let body image control my life. I want to focus on songwriting and feeling healthy and attractive, not on some fictitious, unattainable standard of beauty. Most of all, I don't want to inspire even a single fan who sees my photo in a magazine to think, *I need to look like her to look good.*

When I visit schools and I see girls so anxious, trying so hard, I want to tell them that they are enough, just as they are.

Moby just called from a cell phone. The line was full of static.
   "What?"
   "It was nice hanging out with you yesterday in L.A."
   "What? I can't hear you. The line is cutting out."
   "It was nice singing with you at the Elton John thing yesterday."
   "Oh, yeah—that was fun. Hopefully we'll get to play more together. Where are you?"
   "What?"
   "Where are you?"
   "In Glasgow, on a tour bus."
   "You're in Glasgow already?"
   The phone cut out.

In small, rural towns, stores don't specialize the way they do in bigger cities. A shop might sell, say, chain saws and stationery where another might sell snow skis and goslings. The local taxidermy service might double as a post office. These pairings seem odd to outsiders, but the owners of small-town shops know the needs of small-town people.

As a kid, the Kachemak Bay Grocery and Shoe Store was my favorite. The upper level of the store was always abloom with the usual wilted produce: lettuce; citrus fruit; hard, pink tomatoes—all of it stamped with the weary, dehydrated look that comes from having been shipped a long way from somewhere warm and exotic . . . like Ohio. Downstairs were the shoes. Shoes of every style and sort, but mostly functional shoes that aspired to being somehow fashionable, though those aspirations were seldom fulfilled. But whenever my dad shopped for the basics—flour, sugar, baking soda, chewing tobacco—I'd go downstairs and browse. That's where I first met the photographer.

He had noticed me looking around and decided to say hello. Homer was a friendly place. Usually I tried to be as friendly with the people there as they were with me, but this time I didn't feel so forthcoming. I'm not sure what, but something about the photographer gave me the creeps. I iced him out the best a nine-year-old could.

When my dad walked up, the tone of the conversation lightened. Dad was flattered to hear that the photographer thought I was a beautiful girl. He was even more impressed when the man offered to shoot me for free. In the car on the way home, Dad enthused about how great he thought the offer was. Wasn't I excited? I was not. Nevertheless, Dad made an appointment, and a week later I was scrubbed, shoved into a frilly white dress that was a bit too small, and delivered to the photographer's trailer/studio. Although I was never propositioned or physically threatened, the experience raised goose bumps on my arms. I couldn't wait to get out of there.

On the ride home I told Dad that the photographer gave me a creepy feeling.

"What do you mean, Jewel?"

"Well, he just didn't feel right to me."

"Feel right? But, Jewel, he was very nice."

"I just don't ever want to go back."

My dad was perplexed. And suddenly, I was second-guessing myself. Did Dad believe my feelings were warranted? Who was I, a kid, to suggest there was something "wrong" with an adult? Nothing unusual had been said or happened.

A few months later I was sitting on my bed when my dad came into my room. He had a newspaper in his hands and his eyes were watery. He sat beside me and told me, with utter sincerity and profound emotion, that he was sorry and that he wanted me to always trust my instincts—no matter what.

I wasn't sure what he meant. Then I glanced at the paper in his lap.

There was a picture of the photographer on the front of the *Homer News.* The headline read: POLICE PUT A STOP TO CHILD MOLESTER/PORNOGRAPHER.

⤞

Fame isn't what I thought it would be. Or maybe it is.

When I was living in my car and record labels started approaching me, I was excited, but also scared. The idea of having no privacy seemed unbearable to me, especially as a writer who fed off of observing other people. Touring, being constantly watched and scrutinized, seemed like it would be suffocating to a girl who was raised in Alaska. But it also seemed very worth it. If not for my career, I could never have afforded land to live in Alaska. I would never have been able to perform for such diverse audiences all over the world. And I would never have earned the money to found Higher Ground for Humanity and fund our Clearwater project. It's true, exposure attracts stalkers. I have been afraid at night even in my home. I have had people follow me into rest rooms and wait outside the stall door while I peed so they could get a picture when I came out. But I have also been able to make a living doing something I love. And my fame has made my charitable groups better known. Whether the press shows up for the unveiling of our Clearwater project because it's a good cause or because I'm "Jewel," the organization still prospers. Fame affords me an arena of influence.

As strange and uncomfortable as it all is, it's also very worthwhile. I wouldn't change a thing. Now that I can afford to opt out of the "hit machine"—hell, I can even retire if I want to—I am free to focus on music that is true, music that moves me. All I ever wanted to do was to create honestly, and I am unbelievably blessed to have the luxury to do so.

⤞

Germany

I was walking in a park in Hamburg when I came upon a couple. The woman was younger than me, bundled in a nubby sweater to protect her against the chill of winter. She was pushing a baby in a stroller. The man was not yet thirty but looked very secure, like someone who'd been working most of his life.

I overtook them slowly on a downward slope. As I did, I saw the young mother release the carriage, allowing it to roll ahead of her down the gentle hill. I opened my mouth in a silent warning, but before my words could fully form, she grabbed the handle with her fingertips, just before the carriage moved beyond her reach.

As I passed, she did it again. And again. Each time she watched the carriage roll slightly farther from her. Each time with the strange and desperate smile of a person slipping willingly into a bad dream. It was as if she were deciding whether to let the lifestyle she had chosen roll away from her, down the hill, where she would catch up to it when she felt ready. *If* she ever felt ready.

When she had to quicken her gait, actually take an extra step to capture the stroller, her husband gave her a curious look. She grasped the handle tightly.

But I will always remember the look in her eye—the slow, surreal disbelief of someone who is drowning. And the haunting drama of being an arm's length away from overwhelming happiness, unsure whether to pull it close or let it go.

❧

Maybe today someone will smile at me, not because they recognize me, but just because it's a nice day and they're feeling friendly. Maybe today I won't be suspicious.

❧

San Francisco

Last night the band and I went to a gay club called the Mint. It was karaoke night. Poltz got the emcee to introduce me as Cindy, and the next thing I knew, I was up on the little black stage singing "Foolish Games" into a dinky microphone, Poltz at my side to make sure I'd go through with it. I laughed the whole way through the first verse. But when I got it together and began to sing louder, the room grew quiet.

Is it her? Is it her? I thought he said her name was Cindy? No, I think it's really her.

The smokers got out their lighters and began to sway along silently. I sang along with the lyrics on the TelePrompTer. At the end I read the credits to myself. *Written by Jewel Kilcher, Wiggly Tooth Publishing.* That was my favorite part.

We left quickly amid stunned applause—*Are you Jewel? Are you?*—and caught a cab to a transvestite hangout called Divas. It was talent night. And the local talent was definitely on display. There was a big girl onstage wearing a black miniskirt and a blue sequined bustier accessorized with a large brooch. She was singing a song I did not know. Poltz latched onto a woman whose wig was blond on one side, black on the other. Her large feet were encased in enormous black pumps. Poltz told her that I wanted to sing "Foolish Games," which I didn't, but luckily the club didn't have the CD.

The emcee's name was Ms. October. She was very nice. She introduced me over the mike and before you could say "lipstick" the regulars began dropping by to chat. "What are *you* doing here?" they asked me. Ms. October and a young Asian man named Lou, who manages the club, invited us to the dance club upstairs, but Poltz wanted to watch the last singer, who was belting out a pretty decent rendition of "Tie Me Up."

Once upstairs, in the dance club, I was taken to meet the bartender, who was "such a big fan, he'd die." He was a pretty, thin boy with plucked eyebrows, about twenty-four, in jeans and a white tank top. He told me he was from Anchor Point, Alaska, and that his ex-girlfriend had dated my little brother years ago. Small f-ing world, right? He said it was great to meet me and if I ever needed a really hot-looking drag queen to let him know. I said I would. Then Ms. October, a young thing called Elvira, Poltz, Anna, Brooksie, and I all headed for the dance floor.

I enjoy being a girl. But do I enjoy it as much as Ms. October does?

❧

Once I was at a horse track with Ty and Poltz. I went into the bathroom to pee; a lady in her forties walked in behind me. When she realized who I was, she shrieked at me, "Oh, my!" And she jumped, frightened, like a spider was on her shoulder.

I went into the stall, embarrassed; she took the one next to me, though the room contained about fifteen empty stalls. All was quiet. Then she said, "I just can't believe I'm peeing next to you!"

I froze. There was no way in hell my bladder would function after that.

I couldn't believe it: in the next stall, a woman was actually waiting to hear me urinate.

⁂

Not long ago, when I was visiting Kansas City with a friend, we decided to stop into Houston's Restaurant for dinner. I could see that the restaurant was busy, but I was very hungry, so I walked up to the host and asked shyly, "Room for two?"

He took one look at us and answered curtly, "Sorry. No." So off we went.

My friend and I had walked more than half a block when I stopped in my tracks.

Hey, wait a minute, I thought. *I'm famous now, right? I'm supposed to get tables now! I'm supposed to say to the maître d',* "Do you know who I am?" *And he's supposed to say,* "Oh, yeah. I do. Here. Have a seat. I live solely to make your life more comfortable." But could I actually go through with it?

We considered the possibilities. I've always felt it was silly to use celebrity as an admission ticket, but I was starving. I thought, *What the hell, I'm going to try it.* So we went back to the restaurant.

I was having second thoughts about the whole deal and was about to leave again when I overheard the host deep in conversation with the restaurant manager. His back was to the door—and to me. He was saying, "You wouldn't believe who just came in here. Jewel!"

The manager was a lean man with a slouchy back that made him look like a weasel. He sort of sneered and said, "Oh, yeah? How did you know it was her? Did she have a snaggle tooth?" The joke sent spools of laughter shooting out of him.

Then he walked away into the dining room chuckling, savoring his sharp wit. I was shocked and embarrassed. From across the room I called after him, "What did you say about my tooth?" He never even turned around to face me. He just sort of skipped a half step, then hurried away.

At any rate, we got a table.

The first time I saw a picture of myself on one of those huge billboards on the freeway, it was wild. I looked so out of proportion to myself, like somebody in one of those funhouse mirrors.

The effects of fame are extraordinary. Until you get there, there's just no real way of preparing for it.

I was an eighteen-year-old kid with creativity, talent, and potential. I was also an eighteen-year-old kid who was insecure, highly self-critical, and prone to dark moods of doubt and depression. Fame is like adding fuel to a fire. It develops the creativity and exaggerates the talent but also exacerbates the insecurity. Suddenly, there are more opportunities for self-criticism and greater depths of depression to delve into as well as greater outlets for creativity.

The thing I have had to work on most diligently is correcting these negative tendencies because if they go unchecked they can run rampant. I have had to work hard and stay constantly focused—why am I so hard on myself . . . why do I doubt so often . . . why am I sad?

Without this focus and change in my life, without Nedra and Jacque constantly helping me to figure these things out, I believe I would have lost my way. I would have become more neurotic and self-hating until these emotions eclipsed my talent.

Through the years, I have regained myself. I have also learned to access that miraculous center I lived in so instinctively as a child. It has never been lost. It was only buried. My light wasn't damaged or broken. It was wrapped in layers of doubt and insecurity. Somehow, just knowing that seemed to help a lot. Now it's just a question of remembering what's inside me and acting on it, day by day.

Some days are still more difficult than others.

~

I had heard that if you fast in another person's name, it lends energy to them. I discovered the extent of Jacque's illness while filming *Ride with the Devil* in Missouri. I immediately started fasting, partially in disbelief and partially in total panic. Sensing my distress, the producers were kind enough to give me a few days off from the film to let me visit her.

I arrived in town on May 23 . . . my birthday. I had been warned that Jacque's condition might be startling to me. She had lost a considerable amount of weight since the last time I had seen her—enough to have made it impossible for her to leave the house for weeks. I told her we'd be happy to visit her at her home to make things easier for her, but Jacque insisted: she could make it to the birthday dinner that was being held for me.

I was unprepared for how sick she was. When she came to the private room at the hotel, her pink dress and white cardigan hung on her like on a hanger. She looked so fragile. I couldn't help but burst into tears at the sight of her . . . not just because she appeared ill, but because I had missed her so much while I was in Missouri. I loved Jacque. As much as I loved my own mother. More sometimes than I loved myself. She was constant and kind and wise and always there. I depended on her to explain things to me, such as life and hurt and what I could do better and how I could be more helpful to others. Her life was dedicated to service. To the aid of others. And she had done so much. She was dedicated to helping indigenous people around the world improve living conditions. She worked to integrate their wisdom into modern cultures. She encouraged religious leaders of many nations and theologies to be more tolerant and to see the ultimate unity of all spiritual disciplines. She helped and loved me so much. I was overjoyed to see her.

She sat next to me and delighted in the food, although she could not eat it. And when it was time for the gifts, she oohed and aahed over each one—then she gave me her gift: a gold ring set with diamonds and a long, liquid-blue topaz stone. I knew the ring had belonged to her. There was something about the way she handed it to me that seemed like the passing of a torch. It chilled me. If that was the case, I was not so sure I wanted it, but I slipped it on my finger.

After dinner, Jacque asked me to sing her favorite song. It was one I wrote the previous Christmas, when we were all together in Hawaii. The song was called "Life Uncommon," and when I first played it for her, she wept. She told me, "This is a song of true independence and freedom. I have a feeling there will be a big Fourth of July event next year and you'll play it then. Promise me you will." I promised. There I sat, on my birthday, singing Jacque the freedom song. But none of us felt free. Jacque was throwing up every hour, sometimes more.

I spent my remaining free days at her home, singing to her, praying for her, rubbing her swollen legs and feet, and trying to believe she would get the miraculous healing she so longed for. But it was not to be.

Less than two months later, Jacque was moved to a hospice to die. She weighed seventy-eight pounds. My mom and I joined Jacque's sons and other friends and family in her small hospital room. Jacque had been unconscious for days. But the moment I saw her, her eyes lit up. She became animated, looked straight at me, and smiled. I tried to keep my emotions in check, but on the drive home, I cried as though I'd never stop.

When we arrived at the hospice on the second day, her oldest son greeted me with a hug and a bemused "Happy Fourth of July." It's the Fourth of July? I'd lost track of the days. It gave me a chill in my bones.

We stayed with Jacque all day and into the evening. We sang songs and spoke to her. We took turns stroking her forehead. And then, when her breath grew raspy, we all lit candles and said our good-byes. We told her how much we loved her but that it was okay for her to go on without us. Then we waited silently for her to pass.

As fireworks began to explode in the sky outside the window, Jacque's breath quit coming. We all sat silent. It was over. We joined hands, formed a circle around her bed, and said a prayer. Then her youngest son leaned over and whispered in my ear, "Sing her the song . . . sing her the independence song." I was numb. I didn't know if I could. My voice was trembling and I was shaking and I could hardly stand it. But somehow I found the first words.

Don't worry, Mother, it'll be all right . . .

And then the rest came, as though someone else was singing it. And amid the faint booms and explosions of fireworks, I sang the song just like she asked two months earlier. I grew more certain with each passing phrase that Jacque was still near and would always hear.

We will lend our voices only to sounds of freedom
No longer lend our strength to that which we wish to be free from
Fill our lives with love and bravery
and we will lead lives uncommon . . .

CHAPTER 6

*T*he woman sitting next to me in seat 1-B tells me her brother's pancreas and kidney have failed from diabetes. He awaits a transplant.

A friend is a single father. He used the last of his food stamps two days ago, a week before the beginning of the month.

Suffering is everywhere. Don't think it isn't. So are miracles. Never think they aren't.

Something feels funny, feels unkind
don't worry, soon it'll slip your mind . . .

❧

Rome to Knoxville

Music fills my ears as I depart Rome. Of course, Rome is just the type of place that might cause someone's head to spontaneously fill with music. This ancient city, full of wonders, begs for a good soundtrack. But it's not that type of music I'm hearing right now. What's being pumped into my ears is overly sentimental, pseudoclassical, canned airplane Muzak. This may be the worst thing about airplane travel.

I have been in Rome for a week to sing for the pope. As it turned out, he was quite ill and could not make the performance. I ended up doing two days of rehearsals with some local and international singers, then finally a show for a group of high-ranking clergy from the Vatican.

While I was onstage, I marveled at the sublime beauty of the surroundings. I felt very lucky to see the famed Sistine Chapel. All of the churches I have toured here are so exquisite, they entice the visitor to anticipate the riches of God's heaven.

Such great temples, of every denomination, yet people starve right outside their glittered halls. A mystery of faith.

❧

I am pleased and excited and happy. I love my job. I'm full of ideas and have plenty of time to think of better ones. I'm so thankful for the new songs I've been writing and for the good show last night in Boston. My life gets more exciting with each day that passes.

When I was nineteen or twenty, and first started getting noticed by the press, I have to admit it turned my head. Suddenly, journalists were telling me, "You know, you're such a mature writer for your age!" or "I just can't get your songs out of my head." At that time I was desperate to take all the credit I could get—even from complete strangers. I wanted people to think I was extraordinarily talented—that I could compose without strain, be perfect without effort. Most of all, I wanted to believe it myself. So I sort of smiled and feigned humility and took all the credit anyone wanted to pile on. Why yes, I guess I *was* special! I guess I did embody innate greatness! And did I mention that I could actually levitate?

As soon as my mom read these articles she took me aside. She was well aware of what made me hungry for affirmation. And most of all, she knew that the real reason I got into music had nothing to do with acclaim. She spoke to me frankly.

Was it possible I'd feel dishonest if I shared only my successes rather than my struggles? Wouldn't denying my difficulties simply be contributing to the kind of thinking that made me feel inadequate to begin with?

At first I was offended by her suggestions, but after I took time to reflect I realized Nedra was right. Pretending I was perfect was dishonest and made me feel I had an unreal image of myself to uphold. Nedra wasn't asking me to focus on my tendency to doubt myself and she wasn't saying I didn't deserve compliments; she was encouraging me to align my actions with my intent. I had a choice: I could continue to act on my old, destructive ideas about myself and ignore my feelings of inadequacy or I could view them as opportunities for growth and get a chance to create a life that looked like me in the press rather than a fictitious one.

With Nedra's help I began to live as what I desired myself to be—a person who lived as honestly as possible, full of mistakes and good intentions. My personal problems could easily have sabotaged my creativity and even my career; I could have ended up bitter and unfulfilled. My mother didn't just give me life; she helped me see choice within my life. For this gift alone I will always be grateful for her particular kind of love.

❧

My junior year of high school I came home for Christmas to find Nedra ill. I knew my mother had heart problems, particularly an inherited condition that weakened a major artery in her heart. On Christmas Eve, at my aunt's house, she suffered a small heart attack. There she was, laid out on the floor. I knelt by her feet and looked into her eyes. For some reason, I felt no fear.

"You know, I get your best jewelry if you die," I told her. My joke sent my uncle into spasms of dirty looks, but my mom laughed. She wasn't worried I'd get it. Neither was I. My mom and I had always been deeply connected, and now that she was ill the bond grew even stronger. From that time on I became much more accountable in my relationship with Nedra. I no longer took her for granted. I began to understand her not just like a mother but as a person that I respected and wanted to honor. A person whose respect I wanted to earn beyond our mother-daughter relationship.

The moment of her heart attack was frightening; yet an enduring calm came over me. I knew that Nedra would not leave me. I had a sudden sense that, together, we had a purpose. There was much we would do.

❧

Portland

Higher Ground for Humanity is actually becoming a reality. When we were still living in our cars, Mom and I made a pact that we would both work as hard as we could, and that if we ever made it—and I actually became successful—we'd start a humanitarian organization. It's amazing to see how quickly it has all happened. While I was recording the *Spirit* album, Nedra was busy setting up the organization. One of the first projects HGH will fund is the Clearwater project. We are sending a team of biologists, scientists, and engineers along with a film crew into Honduras, Mexico, Africa, India, and the U.S. to find places that need clean water. We will install the technology and educate the community so that waterborne diseases become eradicated in that area. The tour I'm on now is what will fund this project and make it possible. This is a dream come true. It is my way to make a difference.

◈

Offenbach, Germany

Some nights are so lonely, the stars seem to weep. All things seem to share my sorrow. A woman's laughter rises, smooth as porcelain, then shatters under the burden of its own weight. The chatter that bubbles up from the street to my window falls again, smothered in muffled restraint or hoarse reproaches.

Nedra used to say that I could trust sorrow, like all things, to obey rhythm. All things ebb and flow, move in and out, grow light and dark and light again.

I am a child. I still butcher delicate things with inexperience and good intentions.

◈

When we lived in Seward, my mom suggested that we go to Fairbanks to an Indian gathering. There, I heard many people speak their hearts with profound simplicity and honesty. They weren't embarrassed or shy or ashamed. And more than anything, I longed to do that, too. But when I was asked to speak, I couldn't. I just stood there and panicked because I felt mute, as if my throat were closed and I had no means of expression left to me except my writing. I had written what I felt for so long, I didn't realize how alone and quiet and buried within myself I had become.

A short time later I hiked alone to the top of a nearby mountain. I paused at the summit and collected my thoughts. I tried to say something real—just to the wind. But I could not. I couldn't coax a sound from my lips. It was as though my feelings had frozen inside me, like a small stream, paralyzed by the hand of winter. I wanted so much to feel like I used to, to feel light and free and not stuck inside myself. I would work as hard as I had to to change this.

◈

Munich, Another Hotel

Well, I have to cancel the rest of my European tour. I have hurt my voice. I'm not sure what the deal is exactly, but I can't talk, sing, or breathe without pain. And my ears are plugged. They have been since Australia, really, and that stop was many shows, cities, countries, and at least three continents ago.

I had a local doctor here in Munich look at my throat. He was no specialist, just a general practitioner, and didn't shed too much light on the situation. He told me that I had to sing in Germany because his son had tickets for the show. He also suggested that I might want his son for a boyfriend. The odd thing is, he was serious. Moments later he ushered the awkward seventeen-year-old in and described him to me as a "regular Forrest Gump." I still don't know what that meant.

His medical advice to me was to take a steroid pill. That would shrink the swelling of my vocal cords and enable me to perform. Would I screw up my voice more by doing a show? Could I trust this man? I've had hoarse throats before but nothing like this. The doctor also told me to boil some potatoes, mash them, put them in a wool sock, and use it as a poultice for my throat. Which I did. I'd pee on spark plugs if I thought it would help.

I sang okay at the show (the steroids worked amazingly quickly) but it hurt terribly. I called my mom and asked what I should do. She wanted me off the tour immediately. The doctor thought my plugged ears were a symptom of hearing damage caused by the loud stage volume and the in-ear monitors I wear when I perform. Continued exposure to that kind of stress might be causing my eardrums to protect themselves by swelling and filling with fluid. He said depending on how long it had been happening, I could sustain a slight but permanent hearing loss. I hated canceling the last five shows of the tour but decided it was better than risking my voice and hearing.

So here I am, getting ready to fly to Frankfurt, then to the States.

❧

Moose Lodge, New Zealand

The deck is weathered. The wood is gray and faded from staring out at the sea so long. I imagine this porch has loved the sea from its quiet perch and that the sea, in return, has assaulted it with salt air and sun and weather, causing the bright blond wood to sag and fade with time. To be loved until you come undone at the seams. To be fondled and drenched and bruised and exhausted and exalted by love. Far better this than to grow weary and fragile from never giving in to love.

Tonight the air is damp and the little wooden deck seems to be perched on the edge of endless darkness. I have just returned from the hot mineral pool, which is in an open hut at the edge of the sea. I left the lights off so I might be forced to feel my way to the water in the moonless night. The waters came up from a natural spring and the air smelled of rich sulfur. No noise but my breath and the lapping of water upon the shore. My legs entered the unlit pool like two knives made of flesh. Smooth and quiet, my limbs sliced the water until they disappeared inside of it, as if erased by the aqueous hand of Poseidon himself. I floated, barely breathing, and closed my eyes. I imagined that my head was in the world but that below the surface of the water my body dangled like ghostly roots in the weightless starry black of outer space. The noiseless black of outer space. Slowly, I contracted my limbs into a tight knot around my middle, then I expanded, feeling each muscle lengthen to its greatest capacity. Then, with a rapid swoosh, I contracted again like the pale wing of a butterfly. I spread myself again lazily as if bathing in the sun, languid once again. I held my breath and stared out at the sky. Only my face and the crest of my bosom staring back at the stars.

Chilled, I scuttled back up the path wrapped in a towel, my clothes in a messy bundle in my arms. My posture was laughable, twisted awkwardly in an effort to prevent my wet hair from touching my bare shoulders. My hair did not feel fine and harmless; it had suddenly become cold and heavy as metal. My teeth chattered even as I jumped into the warm robe I now wear.

Now the light I write by shares itself with the porch, bringing it partially out of the darkness, away from its lover. Soon I shall turn out the light and let it be alone with its lovely ocean.

I have no lover to whisper in my ear and smother me in clever kisses. I am left alone with my thoughts, the pen my most constant companion.

Before I recorded "Pieces of You," I thought maybe because I hadn't been trained as a singer I wasn't a "real" singer. So I took a few lessons. The next thing I knew, I was painfully conscious of my vocal cords and consumed with being "correct," which took all of the joy out of performing. The training also made my voice sound funny—like on the album version of "You Were Meant for Me." It just doesn't sound like me. It flowed correctly, and from my diaphragm, but not from my heart.

    Lessons in anything have the potential to homogenize if the focus is on "correctness" rather than self-expression. Self-expression begins and ends with the soul.

Pittsburgh

I'm sitting in a church in Pittsburgh that reeks of fresh paint. The day is hot and still, with no breeze to move the air around. Someone has installed two large fans—one in front of Mary's shrine, another in front of the statue of St. Joseph—to keep the faithful from inhaling the paint fumes and fainting. Did vandals break one of the lovely painted glass windows? One is missing, replaced by a clear glass panel, sealed in plastic. Though few churches here in the U.S. compare with the Gothic masterpieces in Cologne or the Duomo in Florence, this is a lovely church.

    It is between services and there are only three of us here, two elderly ladies and me, sitting on pews that have been hewn from blond spruce. Both ladies have white hair. One lady has a bent back and wears powder blue. The other is sporting large earrings and a navy-blue button-up, smock-type thing. She seems lost, and contented to be so. Anyway, they have come in separately to read Scripture. They steal glances at me as I write.

To my left, an elderly man appears. He pops from behind the statue of the Virgin Mary like a jack-in-the-box. He must work here. He makes the sign of the cross and kneels by the large fan, his head resting on the front of a kneeler. On her way out, the lady in navy blue stops at my pew and smiles. She gives me a booklet with a picture of Jesus on its cover. The title reads, *A Collection of the Thoughts of Padre Pio of Dietrelcina, Italy.* She says, "You can keep this." Then she looks deep into my eyes and adds, "God bless you." She has very kind eyes. "Thank you very much and God bless you, too," I whisper. Maybe she doesn't look so lost after all. Maybe I look lost to her. Alone, with my black glasses propped up on my head, messy blond hair, rumpled black satin pants, Prada shoes, scribbling in a notebook like a madwoman instead of praying.

I lean back against the cool pew. There are confessional booths to my left, against the wall. One door is marked PRIEST. It has a cross above it. The other is wired with a light to tell if it's occupied. My writing is my confessional, I suppose.

I can't believe God cares for rules. Only for the sacred, which is known intrinsically by each heart.

Jacque explained it best.

There was a mountain, she said. At its summit, there burned a great fire. The fire and its energy had created the mountain, and it was what continued to create it, regularly sending streams of molten earth cascading down the mountain's side, where they would cool and harden and, ultimately, sustain life. Then one day, the mighty fire sent out spits of flame that landed in various places on the mountain's side, kindling a number of smaller fires.

There were many groups of people who lived on the mountain, but because the mountain was so large and the people's communities so disparate, these groups of people remained strangers to each other. When they discovered the small fires, the people gathered near them for light and warmth. Each group did what they could to keep their fire alive. And each came to know their fire by a name they could understand. Some called the fire Christianity; another group knew it as Hinduism; another Islam or Tao.

Each camp sought to learn the fire's source. But because the mountain was so large, they could not see that there were other fires hidden in the trees, each as bright and compelling as their own. Nor could they understand that each of these small fires had emanated from the same source . . . a source so expansive it gave birth to itself . . . with as many names to know it by as there were people to know it.

I hope the world religions come to see that their similarities are greater than their differences. I hope to see people stop killing in the name of God.

5/23/99

It is May 23. Another birthday. I was up late in the studio remixing "Jupiter," so I slept until noon. The hotel management heard it was my birthday and so they sent up a chocolate cake with a candle in it. The waiter seemed as embarrassed by the whole thing as I was. "Should I light the candle?" he asked. For a moment I considered the awkwardness of blowing out the single pink birthday candle with the waiter as my sole witness and celebrant. I decided on a more private affair. I declined. The waiter looked relieved, then made his way out of my messy room with head bent. Hotels are curious places. They exist to provide a haven for your most private moments, but since total strangers must service your minibar, they are likely to catch you in a robe, or find your socks strewn about the floor, or glimpse the bra you've flung over a chair to dry after a quick wash in the bathroom sink.

I am in Hyde Park. The day is sunny and so breezy it seems to have blown all of London out of their flats. Families and lovers and flocks of preening teens walk about, play soccer, and lie in the sun. Along the river there are lawn chairs, and so I make my way toward one, only to be waylaid by a young man in green. There is a one-pound charge for the chair, he tells me. I have no pounds. I left the hotel with nothing but my pen and paper, and so I lie now on my side next to the chair and write and watch him patrol the area. Maybe I should have told him it was my birthday, though I doubt he would have believed me, or cared.

My brother Atz is here to visit. It is lovely to have him, though somehow it makes me homesick. I long to lie in the wet grass that is tall and smells still of things new and green, and stare at the sky as the clouds race high above. I long to spend hours this way. Days. Just letting the wind fill my ears and watching my skin grow dark and drenched with sun. But London has become something of a second home to me. In the past year I've spent more time here than I have in San Diego. It has begun to feel familiar to me, out of repetition, if nothing else.

Let's see . . . where did I spend my last birthday? I know. I was in Seattle. Jacque gave me that topaz ring that was the same bright violet as her eyes. The year before? Hmm. I can't remember. Norway maybe, sick with a cold. Yeah, that was it. I know I had the day off because I was sick. I remember being glad I was sick so I could have the day off. This year I have the day off, too. We board the bus for Amsterdam at midnight.

I move to a bench and watch three grown men stop to stare at a fat squirrel as if it were a rare white leopard they had come across on safari. Cameras out. Big smiles plastered on. The clouds are growing thick now, and suddenly, the wind seems a bit less playful. Two women sit next to me on the bench. They speak to each other in thick accents and gesture dully, their arms bundled oddly in thick sweaters.

Both women look ill. One is Spanish. She is wearing very thick glasses and her head is wrapped in a scarf. She is very talkative, frenetically so, like a marionette dancing at the end of her string in an attempt to cheer a jaded audience. She has her work cut out for her. The other lady, who is French, appears to be wasting away. She cannot weigh more than ninety pounds. Her face is green, her hands are green and sharp, like a skeleton's.

Two teenage girls walk by. They are sixteen or seventeen years old. One stares at the French woman with a scowl, making fun of her to her friend. As she walks by me I give her a dirty look. She has made the two women self-conscious; now they sit in silence, staring at their shoes. They are quiet for some time. Then the one with the glasses picks up the tempo again, chattering exaggeratedly in her thick Spanish accent. A friend like that would be good to have.

I spend the rest of my birthday walking the streets of London with Blade and Atz. Later I am lured to a surprise birthday party at the Blue Bird Café, but I leave after the appetizers to catch the end of Springsteen's show, which rocks. I hurry back to the café in time for the cake—all the crew were there, very sweet—head back to the hotel to load luggage on the bus, then, at one A.M., head up the road to the Dorchester to meet the Boss, Sting, and their wives. Very cool. Then my band loaded up and we drove nine hours to Amsterdam. I woke at noon in a hot bus that smelled of leftover bean dip and birthday cake.

❧

Nedra bought Jacque a piece of art in India. They had been to the market together, and while exploring, had come across a shop where a man was selling impossibly beautiful handwoven rugs. The rugs were covered in thousands of intricate stitches and studded with hundreds of jewels that had been sewn right into the weave, so that the entire piece glittered with garnets and tigereye and amethyst and moonstone and jet and tourmaline. Jacque immediately fell in love with a black rug on which a vase of bright flowers had been embroidered in shining silk thread. While she exclaimed excitedly about the craftsmanship, about the way the thread cast the light this way then that, and about how it had taken someone ten years to create this work of genius, Nedra bought the rug for her in secret.

When Nedra presented the rug to Jacque, back in the States, she was elated. But Jacque never got a chance to hang the rug. We have it now, and we've not hung it either.

❧

5/3/00
Today in the mail I received a birthday present from a fan— two gift certificates to McDonald's. One for Nedra and one for me.

❧

When I was eighteen and living with my mom in Poway, California, I went through a sort of premature midlife crisis. Or maybe what I went through was something every eighteen-year-old faces and I was just more dramatic about the whole thing. At any rate, I felt a terrible sense of emptiness, as though I had no purpose, no reason to live. When I envisioned my life stretching out before me, I saw myself passing time. Work, eat, sleep—for what? I imagined myself raising a family and that didn't make me feel fulfilled. I needed a purpose. Between shifts of temporary jobs, I sat alone and tried to figure out what kind of life would make me want to be conscious every day. I felt I must have been put here for a reason. I wanted to know what that reason might be.

When I told my mom how I felt, she said that as soon as I figured out what I wanted to do she'd do what she could to help me. I told her that I wanted something different from going to college, seeking a career, or having a family; I wanted to make a difference in people's lives, in the world. Visualizing myself in that role made me feel calm inside. But how could I reach that goal? I wasn't sure I could help myself, much less other people. Nevertheless, I was excited. At last, I was onto something that filled me with hope.

My mom helped me to clarify my ideas. She said that my desire to help was great, but in what way would I bring about change? Becoming an environmental lawyer, a teacher, or a good mom were all choices that made a difference in the world. I decided that my writing and singing talents were among the things I could bring to the table.

I knew that I felt less alone when I sang because music allowed me to share my feelings with others. Some of the people who came to my shows had told me that they felt less isolated when they listened to my songs. My lyrics reassured them that someone else had experienced the same emotions, walked the same path as they did. That settled it. I told my mom that I knew what I wanted to do. I wanted to write songs and sing for people. I asked her if she could help me make some demo tapes. She said she would—but there was one more factor to consider. In order for my dream to be realized, it was important for me to know what had attracted me to that dream. Why did I want a music career? Were there reasons for my decision beyond wanting to help?

Again, I sat alone. This time, I wrote about those things that intrigued me about music—and those that did not. Beyond the sheer love of performance, the hope that a music career would bring money and excitement and fame seemed to be an obvious plus. But when I projected into the future, visualizing a life of only money and notoriety, my feeling of internal calm faded away. Wealth and attention as goals would never sustain me through a challenging career. Whatever happened, I knew I would not be satisfied unless my every deal, decision, contract, and performance grew from my deep desire to make a difference rather than prosper financially. I wanted my career to match my intentions and integrity.

My mom and I decided then that when we were able, we would use the money from my success to found Higher Ground for Humanity, our nonprofit organization. And, after only five years, we were able to. It has been a dream come true—a reward that makes all the touring and hard work worth it.

I am on a path, and in a career, where many have lost their footing. I feel in my heart that taking the time to be clear in the beginning, to think about what I wanted from the record industry, has kept me from losing my way. I have a life I feel good in. I have abundance, and I am able to bring abundance and health to others. That's as good as it gets.

A Park in Spain, 11:00 p.m.

Music escapes through an open window, finding its way to me in the night as if the trees themselves conjured each lonely refrain from the shared heart of their mottled limbs. I sit beneath a tree, afraid of bugs I do not know the names of, but not afraid enough to leave. In the distance, I can see a faint orange light. I fancy it is the open window that spills out music. Inside I imagine lovers eating a late dinner. Or maybe a woman alone. Or maybe only a dog is home, left with a CD playing for company.

The night is damp. I pull my collar around my ears and place both hands in small fists beneath my chin. I stare into the darkness.

The forest dances around me to the waltz carried on the breeze. The whole sky begins to sway. I stand, imagining I am in a ballroom. I close my eyes as I dance slowly, swaying like a child, or a woman lost in her lover's arms. The smell of damp earth and pine and wet rocks romances me.

Life romances me often, I think to myself, *though often I do not notice the rhythm or beauty or music that laces all of life with its common thread. Even on the road.*

I must remember this.

⮞

In the music business, everyone wants the artist to keep making money for them, and you're a has-been if your single doesn't fly. During "You Were Meant for Me," I was opening for Neil Young, and recording some new music in my spare time. I had just taken so much criticism for being "too folkie," and "not edgy enough," that I recorded a record that was defensive in direct response. I wanted nothing but hits, I decided. I wanted to be universally liked. On my new record, there was one song that everyone agreed was hit material. The trouble was, I hated the song. It was a good single but it wasn't good music. The label loved it. It embarrassed me. I didn't know what to do. When I told Neil about it, he gave me the best advice. "Jewel, you've probably already sold more records than I have in my entire career. But I sell out sheds consistently. Music isn't about hits; it's about doing what you believe in." While I doubted his humble sales figures, the point hit home.

Another time I opened for Neil and Crazy Horse at Madison Square Garden in New York City. I was nervous to be in New York, playing such a huge venue solo, and opening for a rock band. Neil calmed me down. "Hey, it's just another hash house on the road to success; show them no respect." I don't know if he ever knew how much those small comments meant to me, but at a time when I was unsure, they helped solidify the rules: always believe in the craft of songwriting and in myself above all else . . . disregard the artificial popularity contest and never allow it to dilute my art and muddle my instincts . . . and, finally, don't be too afraid to fall out of favor. Expect it.

Long careers, in or out of music, are made up of dry spells and creative windfalls. Finding a catchy formula might work for one or two songs, but if I quit this business tomorrow what I learned from Neil would still hold true in any field.

⊸≈⊷

Bucking Bulls, Stephenville, TX

Around six o'clock, Ty and I drove over to a man's house in a quiet neighborhood with a dirt street. We were on a mission of mercy. We were going to give a Charolais bull one last chance to buck before he got sold for hamburger.

The Charolais had been ridden once, a few days ago, to see if he could make it as a professional bucking bull. He wasn't that great. But since some bulls grow into a good ride, we were going to give him a second chance. I couldn't help but think that if the bull knew how much was riding on his bucking, he might be sure to kick and spin some.

We turned off the main road where half-run-down houses gathered in a drunken row. Suddenly, we came upon a small corral containing four bucking chutes, fenced with rusty pipes. A black bull waited in one chute; the buff-colored Charolais languished in a pen beyond. A homemade sign hung with twine above one end of the arena proclaimed this place to be RUSTY'S RODEO. A plastic banner informed us that this was also an OFFICIAL SITE AND MEMBER OF THE JUNIOR RODEO LEAGUE. DEDICATED TO THE PERPETUATION OF YOUTH. Did youth need perpetuating? In such a dangerous sport anything hinting at longevity is certainly welcome.

We climbed out of the pickup to join four sweaty cowboys, the nervous black bull in the chutes, the Charolais in the pen, and four tireless kids who ran and played without regard to the oppressive heat. While Ty sized up the guy who was going to ride the bulls, I found a seat beneath a homemade canopy of dry brush and blue visqueen. The three boys and a girl sat on a plywood perch that was high enough to give them a good view over the fence. The oldest boy was full of advice for the rider. "Bear down, Uncle Jake," he'd call. Then he'd spit self-importantly into the dirt. "Just keep in the center, Uncle Jake." The way this ten-year-old kept on, I expected him to jump into the chute himself and show Uncle Jake how the hell it was done.

Down below, Uncle Jake rosined his glove and pulled the rope tight. He looked nervous to be riding in front of Ty Murray, *the* seven-time world champion all-around cowboy. It could have been the heat, but he looked to be sweating just a little more than the other guys. He nodded his head and the black bull bucked out of the gate. The cowboy made it about four seconds despite his nephew's hollers of expert encouragement.

He picked himself off the dirt, grabbed his rope, and went to get ready for his next ride. Ty said to him in a flat tone, "You got your motor runnin' this time?" The cowboy laughed self-consciously at the needling.

If the bull isn't ridden and helped, it's hard to get an idea of what he can do. Then riding him will be a waste of time.

They loaded the Charolais into the third chute. It looked nervous and confused. It tried jumping up over the first gate and almost made it.

The boy called out, "Is the chute broke? Hey, Uncle Jake . . . you ridin' him? Who's ridin' him? Whoever's ridin' him better bear down." No one replied.

When the bull settled, Ty jumped in the chute to tie a rope across the bars. That would keep the Charolais from jumping up again. He rested his knees on the animal's massive back like I'd kneel on the carpet in front of the TV. If the bull acted up before he finished, he'd simply hover above the bull like a gymnast doing warm-ups on lateral bars. When he finished he swung up and over the chute and landed cat-like on his feet in the dusty arena. Then Uncle Jake lowered in to put on his rope.

Once the gate was finally pulled open, the bull seemed confused, like it took him a minute to figure out that the only way out was sideways. After he was out he bucked okay. Better than the first time, they said. The men whooped and hollered trying to provoke the bull and Jake managed to stay on to the buzzer. Once the rider was off, the bull didn't try to charge anyone, which seemed to discourage Ty. Maybe the bull just didn't have fight in him. Ty went in the ring and stepped in front of the Charolais, tempting him. The bull just snorted through his nose and looked at the angry red scrapes on his back end. That's what you get for fussing in the chutes.

The men discussed the bull's improvement. He had done better. Maybe he'd buck better still if they tried him a third time. "Looks like you got a few more days before your ass is hamburger," I overheard one call from behind the chutes.

Bull riding is a man's sport. You earn your way into it with sweat and balls and an inexplicable need to pit your ability against the will of large murderous animals. Whenever I'm around rough stock riders, I'm quite aware I'm not in their club.

I sat alone in the hot air, listening to the boys badger the men for details—*Is he a good bull? Did you like the way he bucked? Did Uncle Jake cover him?*—and did what I could to keep the fire ants from biting my feet through my sandals.

⁂

Some people are lucky if they're good at one thing. My dad was accomplished at two. But he had a family to raise. Now, in his fifties, he's realized that these two talents are the only things that really matter. Now that all us kids are doing fine on our own, my dad's life is spent making music and riding.

In the summers, Dad is like a kid. He never spends a night indoors; he's always in the flatlands of Fox River Valley on his stud, Black Fog, roaming the mountains and valleys. Drinking from streams. Cooking on a fire. Writing songs about the land he calls home and the creatures he calls family. My dad is a cowboy with a poet's heart.

Recently I went home to visit him. When he picked my friend and me up at the airport, he was wearing a T-shirt with the sleeves cut off.

His arms were toned and muscular and tan. He had traded in his black boots for running shoes, his old straw hat for a dark brown beaver felt. The woman with him was like him—athletic, lean, outgoing.

He had a horse trailer hitched to his pickup truck, with two horses waiting patiently. Two more were tethered and waiting at the head of the bay. We got our bags but skipped going to the cabin. We drove straight to the horses so we could spend five of my six free days beneath the stars, sharing the land we love with the ones we love. We had come full circle, my old man and me. In the end, the difficult relationship we'd shared gave way to love. How could it not? Our two common passions, horse riding and music, eclipsed all else until love was all we shared.

When we got camp settled and the horses staked out, my dad pulled out his guitar and said, "Hey, frog bait, I wrote a new song. It may be my best one yet . . . but I'll let you be the judge." I listened happily. This time I had my own songs to play for him.

I return home, a songwriter and a woman. But still, more than ever, I am my father's child.

⊷

I remember we ran a hose from a creek under our house and up through our sink. If it rained hard, the little creek would flood full of white worms with black furry heads. We tied one of my pretty pink scarves onto the mouth of the faucet with a rubber band and used it as a filter. When too many worms collected, we'd unwind the rubber bands, pull the scarf off, empty the little pouch of worms in the slop bucket, which we later fed the chickens, then tie the scarf back on the faucet.

Do you remember, Shane, how we'd bleed a birch tree to collect its sap to make syrup? The trees looked so curious with the little spigots we'd hammered into them—like the forest grew faucets. We'd hang buckets off of them and they'd fill, drop by drop. Then we'd boil it down. But I can't remember if we'd add sugar or not. I just can't remember . . .

⊷

A Bedtime Story

Once Jacque shared with me her favorite bedtime story. It was told to her as a child. I think of it often on nights alone.

It is a magical evening. The air is crisp, potent. A night breeze tugs at your shirtsleeves, beckoning you outside. There, the light of the moon casts a silver path at your feet. You want to follow.

You step into the yard. The evening sky wraps itself around you like a velvet tunnel. The universe beyond opens to you like an endless room, filled with stars and trees and streams. You wish so much to be out there, swimming in the perfumes of midnight, that suddenly your wishes deliver you . . . and magically, you find yourself transported to a small clearing where the grass is wet and silver with dew. At your feet is a trail of stones whose faces are so smooth that the moonlight reflects off them like a thousand tiny mirrors, and fills your eyes with the cool glow of moonbeams. As you step onto that path, you begin to feel as if your feet have tiny wings. You begin to feel lighter and lighter, until you realize the path is not made of stones at all, but innumerable puddles of light. Nor is the path bound by the contours of the earth or by the law of gravity. It is carrying you up. You are climbing into the sky.

You know you are safe, so you proceed unafraid and incredibly excited until another feeling sweeps over you as well: awe. Now you can see beyond the limits of your house, your street, your town . . . beyond the tops of the swaying trees, beyond carved valleys and pale streams. Now, for the first time, you can see a pattern emerging, in the craggy vertebrae of a mountain's back . . . in the brilliant threads of a spider's web that connects rivers to oceans. Can it be that our houses and lives lie scattered on the earth like bright, ageless constellations? And entire forests sway to the same wind?

And then something peculiar happens as you look deeper into the sky above you. You begin to feel burdened by a weight in your chest. Your heart feels heavy, aching with the remembrance of daily life and its density . . . of the dull solidity that keeps us from walking on moonbeams. You are wishing for a cure for this heavy heart when there . . . you see it . . . a chamber, hidden in the sky, veiled in shrouds that have been woven of the fibrous dusk itself. You enter the silvery room.

Three elixirs magically appear before you. Each is contained in a translucent vial: one, ruby pink; one, cobalt blue; and the last, gold. Each hums and vibrates to a tone you cannot hear. Immediately, you understand. You may take any elixir you choose for your heavy heart. You begin to ponder your decision.

What if I take nothing? you ask yourself. *Will my condition be worse than it is now? What if the elixir I choose doesn't work? May I choose again?* You look to the moon and ask, *What is the most potent elixir of all?* Suddenly the evening grows even more still, leaning back on itself like a man, pleased and full, after a satisfying meal. And deep inside you you hear a voice, the voice of your own wise spirit. "Faith," it says. "Faith is the most potent elixir of all. There is no weight faith will not lighten."

You understand. Still you wonder: *How will I remember this and never forget?*

Again the quiet voice of your spirit speaks to you in its wordless way. "The moon will always remind you. All you need do is stand beneath its silver light and you will know that the antidote to doubt, fear, and every earthly ill is always within your reach. But for now, sleep, little one. You will wake in the morning anew."

~

I finally saw a throat specialist here in the States who said that because I've had bronchitis (for the last nine months, along with the plugged ears), my vocal cords have been irritated by the infected mucus from my lungs. They've been exposed to the infection for months. He also said my hearing will heal if I turn the volume down onstage and take a break soon. When I explained that I had to do the Leno show, he recommended that I cancel and allow my voice to rest. He was concerned because he found prenodules on my vocal cords that would become permanent if I continued to sing, potentially damaging my voice. I told him that I had to finish the Christmas tour. He sort of shrugged and gave me more steroids, promising that they would relieve my symptoms long enough for me to do the show that night. Sure enough, my voice worked long enough to sing on *The Tonight Show,* but the swelling came back the minute the medication wore off.

The holidays are nearly here and I'll be singing "Ave Maria" for a month. I have to make it through all the TV shows plus *A White House Christmas Special.* I'm trying not to take the steroids unless I really need to. The doctor gave me antibiotics for my chest. He said that the black/green mucus I've been coughing up is symptomatic of pneumonia. He wants me to cancel the tour, but I can't.

I want this record to do well.

❧

There is a voice you can hear when you're still
it tells you everything you need to know
it's a seed it's a whisper it lights
a darkened room it says

more than the rivers
more than the sea
more than the mountains
and all the valleys

This is your home

in breathes life into your lungs
a single breath connecting
like a silver thread
love to sorrow, joy to dread

more than the rivers
more than the sea
more than the mountains
and all the valleys

This is your home
This is your home
          free

❧

I slept seventeen hours last night, from midnight until five-thirty this evening, and now my body has no clue what time it is. I didn't get hungry for breakfast until nine P.M. My body isn't sure if it's still in Japan or not. I woke up in shock, not sure what state/country/room I am in . . . if the loo is to the left or on the right.

It is a strange thing to stop traveling . . . to come home.

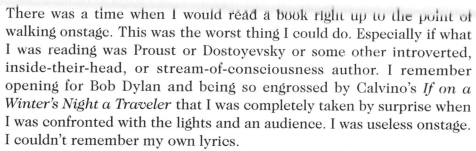

There was a time when I would read a book right up to the point of walking onstage. This was the worst thing I could do. Especially if what I was reading was Proust or Dostoyevsky or some other introverted, inside-their-head, or stream-of-consciousness author. I remember opening for Bob Dylan and being so engrossed by Calvino's *If on a Winter's Night a Traveler* that I was completely taken by surprise when I was confronted with the lights and an audience. I was useless onstage. I couldn't remember my own lyrics.

Now I've banned reading two hours prior to a show. Instead I listen to some Hendrix or hip-hop or the Stones, then just before I go on, I pray. The word "prayer" can seem either ambiguous or strictly attached to some specific ideology. For me, prayer is a time for acknowledgment and gratitude. I find it helps focus my mood for being onstage.

What I love most about performing is that it is constantly my teacher. But what I love most about music is its power to transform. Time and again I have been surprised by music's ability to heighten or alter not only my own mood or outlook, but also that of an entire audience. This is the gift of music: people gather, music is shared, and what transpires between performer and audience somehow becomes greater than either's expectations.

Let me sit here a moment with nothing to do. No interview. No questions about my childhood or what makes me write or is my real name Jewel. Let me sit here and not think about sales or am I too commercial. Let me not think about my backache or shall I fix my tooth or what to do about the fingernail polish that is chipping. Let me just sit here. Quiet. Listen to the hum of midday. To the ocean at my door. To the sound of the world that doesn't recognize faces or even deeds but simply exists.

I feel most at home in two places. One is onstage. To be onstage and sing brings me to life in a way that just can't happen anywhere else. It fills me with awe. The other place, of course, is within nature.

The hills and quiet expanses of Alaska have been my homeland. This extends now to the natural world at large. Anyplace I can be alone in my church of trees, blue skies, river and meadow, ocean and starry night, I feel whole and at peace.

In my present life I find making a retreat into the heart of nature to be not only rejuvenating but also necessary. It helps me experience myself as I know myself to be—a woman and a child who has turned her ear to the wind often to listen.

Even tonight as I walk behind my hotel in the near dark of evening, through a wooded path to find my way to the edge of a lake, I access again all the wonder and wisdom that is offered constantly as a gift from the natural world. It takes me back to the untamed days of my youth, the days spent in the company of my horse roaming mountains and forests, and helps me remain connected to the values of my past. Nature lends me a continuity that threads together the way my life was with the way it is becoming.

I love my present life. I love all the people I meet all over the world. I am constantly in awe of the tenderness and longing and raw human drama I am blessed to come across daily, whether on the city streets of Singapore or the back roads outside of New Orleans.

Essentially this is what we are, lives evolving in tandem with the earth, in harmony with spirit. Old souls that sing their ancient stories and become new with every sunrise. In the coldest darkness. In the irrepressible Texas dawn. In every leaf and sigh.

⇌

Sitting in My Garden

It is all rhythm, I suppose. Not just my music, but my life. Not just my life, but all life. Even the one life we all share.

Like cycles of nature, my own life has rhythms. I am beginning to see and understand these patterns as they are revealed in relationships, childhood, womanhood, career, and creativity. Dissatisfaction, longing, revolution, deliverance. Winter, spring, summer, and fall.

I keep expecting to arrive, as if there were a final destination within me that would be magically unchanging, but there is no such thing. I will want to grow again. My sense of contentment and peace will continually give way to a hunger and desire to move beyond my bounds.

Following a long period of development—of writing music, recording, touring, making a movie, writing this book—I grew concerned as my passion for my profession began to wane. But it wasn't my creativity leaving me; it was the rhythm of my life speaking to me. The act of being alive is a dynamic force. It has a life of its own. It has quiet periods when the fields are fallow and I do not write, time when I must be still. I began to experience great turbulence when I ignored that need and forced myself into constant productivity and movement.

I found myself reevaluating my life this year in a way similar to the time when I lived in my car. *Why was I here? What did I want out of life? What fulfills me and gives me a sense of purpose? Why was I doing all this?* I was frustrated to be circling back around, asking the same questions again. Gradually I began to see the difference. The rhythm is not a circle, it is a spiral. I am in an upward spiral in my life. With each upward spiral I gather maturity, knowledge, skill. I grow in my ability to externally express the transformation that I gain inwardly. This process allows me to return to a season familiar to me and to assess what I've gained, what I've earned, and what it is that I now bring into a new year, and into a new revolution of the spiral.

Everything changes, but as it changes there is one immutable thing and that is the larger rhythm. The rhythm of all that is. It is a rhythm I sense when I turn inward to wonder, or when I lie beneath a tree to watch the leaves sway to the silent music of the wind. The greatest peace I know is in that rhythm. Not fighting it. Listening for what time it is now and knowing that what is empty will soon be full again.

photo credits

Photograph by
Lenedra Carroll

Photograph by
Lenedra Carroll

Photograph by
Lenedra Carroll

Courtesy of
Kilcher family

Photograph by
Lenedra Carroll

Photograph by
Lenedra Carroll

Courtesy of
Kilcher family

Photograph by
Lenedra Carroll

Photograph by
Lenedra Carroll

Photograph by
Wm. Wakeland
Courtesy of
Kilcher family

Photograph by
Lenedra Carroll

Photograph by
Lenedra Carroll

Photograph by
Lenedra Carroll

Photograph by
Lenedra Carroll

Photograph by
Lenedra Carroll

Photograph by
Lenedra Carroll

Photograph by
West Kennerly

Photograph by
West Kennerly

≈

Photograph by
Mairiis Kilcher

Photograph by
Ty Murray

Photograph by
Jewel Kilcher
All photographs in the
photos i've taken section
are by Jewel Kilcher

≈

Photograph by
Ty Murray

Photograph by
West Kennerly

Photograph by
Dylan Davidson

Photograph by
West Kennerly

Photograph by
Lenedra Carroll

Photograph by
Dylan Davidson

Photograph by
West Kennerly

Photograph by
West Kennerly

Photograph by
Lenedra Carroll

Photograph by
Lenedra Carroll

Photograph by
Michel Francoeur

Photograph by
Sean Penn

Photograph by
West Kennerly

Photograph by
Michel Francoeur

Photograph by
Bibi Bielat

Photograph by
West Kennerly

Photograph by
Adrian Green

Photograph by
Sean Penn

Photograph by
Lenedra Carroll

Photograph by
Sheila Kenny

Photograph by
Sean Penn

Photograph by
Sean Penn

Photograph by
Scott Van OpDorp

Photograph by
Bibi Bielat

Photograph by
Keith Anderson

Photograph by
Lee Greene

Photograph by
Keith Anderson

Photograph by
West Kennerly

Photograph by
Sharon Walker

Photograph by
West Kennerly
Photographed on
location of the
Down So Long
music video shoot
directed by
Lawrence Carroll

Photograph by
West Kennerly
Photographed on
location of the
Down So Long
music video shoot
directed by
Lawrence Carroll

Photograph by
West Kennerly

Photograph by
West Kennerly

Photograph by
West Kennerly
Photographed on
location of the
Foolish Games music
video shoot directed by
Matthew Rolston
Jewel is riding Phantom,
owned by
Davida Oberman and
Smokey Robinson